TEXTBOOK OF BLUE BIOTECHNOLOGY

Dr. D.R. Khanna
Reader in Zoology
Gurukul Kangri University
Haridwar
(Uttaranchal)
(India)

D P H

DISCOVERY PUBLISHING HOUSE PVT. LTD.
NEW DELHI-110 002

First Published - 2010

Reprinted - 2018

ISBN: 978-81-8356-554-7

Textbook of Blue Biotechnology

Published by:

DISCOVERY PUBLISHING HOUSE PVT. LTD.

4383/4B, Ansari Road, Darya Ganj

New Delhi-110 002 (India)

Phone: +91-11-23279245, 43596064-65

Fax: +91-11-23253475

E-mail: discoverypublishinghouse@gmail.com

sales@discoverypublishinggroup.com

web: www.discoverypublishinggroup.com

Printed at:

Infinity Imaging Systems

Delhi

Preface

The term 'blue biotechnology' has been used to describe the marine and aquatic applications of biotechnology, but its use is relatively rare. Biotechnology is technology based on biology, especially when used in agriculture, food science, and medicine. Of the many different definitions available, the one formulated by the UN Convention on Biological Diversity is one of the broadest:

> "Biotechnology means any technological application that uses biological systems, living organisms, or derivatives thereof, to make or modify products or processes for specific use."

Biotechnology can also be defined as the manipulation of organisms to do practical things and to provide useful products. One aspect of biotechnology is the directed use of organisms for the manufacture of organic products (examples include beer and milk products. For another example, naturally present bacteria are utilized by the mining industry in bioleaching. Biotechnology is also used to recycle, treat waste, clean up sites contaminated by industrial activities (bioremediation), and produce biological weapons.

There are also applications of biotechnology that do not use living organisms. Examples are DNA microarrays used in genetics and radioactive tracers used in medicine.

Red biotechnology is applied to medical processes. Some examples are the designing of organisms to produce antibiotics, and the engineering of genetic cures through genomic manipulation.

Biotechnology is often broken down into several distinguishing categories, including red biotechnology, which is applied to medical processes, white biotechnology, also known as grey biotechnology which deals with industrial processes, green biotechnology which applies to agricultural processes, and blue biotechnology, which deals with the marine and aquatic applications of biotechnology.

Biotechnology is now one of the fastest growing industries in the world. From controversial stem cell research and revolutionary medical vaccines that save hundreds of lives everyday, to innovative new methods of recycling and harvesting energy to help in the ongoing effort of preserving our environment, the production of synthetic hormones from genetically engineered bacteria and chemical-free organic foods that are helping people to lead healthier lives, biotechnology is forever changing the way we all live our lives.

Author

Contents

1

Introduction

The term 'blue biotechnology' has been used to describe the marine and aquatic applications of biotechnology, but its use is relatively rare. Biotechnology is technology based on biology, especially when used in agriculture, food science, and medicine. Of the many different definitions available, the one formulated by the UN Convention on Biological Diversity is one of the broadest:

> "Biotechnology means any technological application that uses biological systems, living organisms, or derivatives thereof, to make or modify products or processes for specific use."

Biotechnology can also be defined as the manipulation of organisms to do practical things and to provide useful products. One aspect of biotechnology is the directed use of organisms for the manufacture of organic products (examples include beer and milk products. For another example, naturally present bacteria are utilized by the mining industry in bioleaching. Biotechnology is also used to recycle, treat waste, clean up sites contaminated by industrial activities (bioremediation), and produce biological weapons.

There are also applications of biotechnology that do not use living organisms. Examples are DNA microarrays used in genetics and radioactive tracers used in medicine.

'Red biotechnology' is applied to medical processes. Some examples are the designing of organisms to produce antibiotics, and the engineering of genetic cures through genomic manipulation.

White biotechnology, also known as grey biotechnology, is biotechnology applied to industrial processes. An example is the designing of an organism to produce a useful chemical. White biotechnology tends to consume less in resources than traditional processes used to produce industrial goods.

'Green biotechnology' is biotechnology applied to agricultural processes. An example is the designing of transgenic plants to grow under specific environmental conditions or in the presence (or absence) of certain agricultural chemicals. One hope is that green biotechnology might produce more environmentally friendly solutions than traditional industrial agriculture. An example of this is the engineering of a plant to express a pesticide, thereby eliminating the need for external application of pesticides. An example of this would be Bt corn. Whether or not green biotechnology products such as this are ultimately more environmentally friendly is a topic of considerable debate.

Bioinformatics is an interdisciplinary field which addresses biological problems using computational techniques. The field is also often referred to as computational biology. It plays a key role in various areas, such as functional genomics, structural genomics, and proteomics, and forms a key component in the biotechnology and pharmaceutical sector.

Biotechnology Information

Biotechnology is defined as the use of living organisms and other biological systems to manufacture drugs and other products for the purposes of environmental management and/or for the betterment of individual and societal health and well-being.

The practice of biotechnology has been around for centuries, gradually helping our society to evolve into what we have today. From the first moment man realized that he could grow his own crops to sustain the life of his family and community, biotechnology began. When it was discovered that cream could be churned into butter, or that grapes could be fermented into wine, biotechnology was in full practice.

Biotechnology is often broken down into several distinguishing categories, including red biotechnology, which is applied to medical processes, white biotechnology, also known as grey biotechnology which deals with industrial processes, green biotechnology which applies to agricultural processes, and blue biotechnology, which deals with the marine and aquatic applications of biotechnology.

It is now one of the fastest growing industries in the world. From controversial stem cell research and revolutionary medical vaccines that save hundreds of lives everyday, to innovative new methods of recycling and harvesting energy to help in the ongoing effort of preserving our environment, the production of synthetic hormones from genetically engineered bacteria and chemical-free organic foods that are helping people to lead healthier lives, biotechnology is forever changing the way we all live our lives.

There is much talk about 'Biotechnology'. It even turned into a part of out routine chats. Biotechnology is one of the most emerging carrier opportunities in India as well as abroad. There were tremendous improvements in output from the biology section in the past one decade. The surfacing of new technologies also contributed a lot. The developments in full genome sequencing project under takings, comprising human genome, have resulted in engendering very large data.

There are sub fields here also. Few are noted as Red Biotechnology which can be practical to medical processes. Say making organisms suitable to manufacture antibiotics, and the engineering of genetic cures to heal diseases using 'genomic manipulation'. White Biotechnology, (also grey biotechnology), is biotechnology applied to industrial processes. Say using an organism to produce a useful chemical. The next in this group is *Green Biotechnology* which is generally useful to agricultural processes. *Bioinformatics* is another field allied to Biotechnology which generally addresses biological problems deploying computational techniques (also called computational biology). It takes part in a vital character in various areas like structural genomics, functional genomics, and proteomics. Another is blue biotechnology, which is application of Biotechnology in the marine and aquatic division.

There are so many institutes who offer courses (and jobs too – in research field and teaching position). The main institutes who offer research assistance in India include Centre for DNA Fingerprinting and Diagnostics (CDFD), Hyderabad ; Institute of Bioresources and Sustainable Development (IBSD), Imphal, Manipur ; Institute of Life Sciences, Bhuvaneswar ; National Institute Of Immunology, New Delhi ; National Centre For Plant Genome Research (NCPGR), JNU, New Delhi ; National Brain Research Centre (NBRC), Gurgaon ; National Centre for Cell Sciences, Pune . In the public sector undertaking side the leaders are Bharat Immunologicals & Biologicals Corporation Limited, Bulandshahar and Indian Vaccines Corporation Limited, Gurgaon.

Hardly the younger generation understands that India was the first nation to institute (in 1987) a Biotechnology Information System (BTIS) network to craft an infrastructure that facilitates it to harness, "biotechnology through the application of Bioinformatics". The Department of Biotechnology (DBT) says: "BTIS is today recognized as one of the major scientific network in the world dedicated to provide the-state-of-the-art infra-structure, education, manpower and tools in bioinformatics." It further states "The principal aim of the bioinformatics programme is to ensure that India emerges as a key international player in the field of bioinformatics; enabling a greater access to wealth of information created during the post-genomic era and catalyse the country's attainment of lead position in medical, agricultural, animal and environmental biotechnology. India should create a niche in Bioinformatics industry and would work to create bioinformatics industry with turnover of US$ 5 billion by the end of 10th Plan period."

2

Importance of Marine Wealth

INTRODUCTION

India is endowed with a long coastline and hence offers scope for large exploitation of marine wealth. Till a few years back, fishermen in India were involving themselves in traditional marine fishing. In the seventies fishermen started concentrating on catching prawns more commonly known as 'shrimps' due to high profitable return on the same on account of their export value. Brackish water prawn farming started in a big way during 91-94 especially in the coastal districts of Andhra Pradesh and Tamil Nadu. Subsequently due to disease problems, litigation in supreme court and other social and environmental problems the sector suffered a huge set back and most of the corporate farms were closed. However, the small units continued to do farming and adopting extensive prawn farming systems. The shrimp farming has now been regulated with the establishment of Aquaculture Authority of India as per directions of Supreme Court for issuing licenses and overall supervision. It is commonly said that after Green and White Revolution in India, it is time for Blue Revolution to exploit the huge potential in fisheries sector. Shrimps are called the "Pinkish Gold" of the sea because of its universal appeal, unique taste, high unit value and increasing demand in the world market.

Scope for Brackish Water Shrimp Farming

The over exploitation of shrimp from natural sources and the ever increasing demand for shrimp and shrimp products in the world market has resulted in the wide gap between the demand and supply shrimp in the International market. This has necessitated the need for exploring new avenues for increasing prawn production. The estimated brackish water area suitable for undertaking shrimp cultivation in India is around 11.91 lakhs ha. spread over 10 states and union territories viz... West Bengal, Orissa, Andhra Pradesh, Tamil Nadu, Pondicherry, Kerala, Karnataka, Goa, Maharashtra and Gujarat. Of this only around 1.2 lakhs ha. are under shrimp farming now and hence lot of scope exists for entrepreneurs to venture into this field of activity. The following table gives the state-wise potential and present level of development as on March 1996.

Location of the Project

The first and foremost requirement for entering into this venture is the acquisition of suitable land. The details of land identified/surveyed in coastal districts are available with the department of fisheries of the concerned State Governments and with the Regional offices of the MPEDA functioning in the coastal states of India. A suitable site is one that can support optimum conditions for the growth of shrimps at targetted production level. Most of the lands available along the coastline are owned by the State Governments. In some cases, the entrepreneur has to get it on long term lease from the revenue authorities of the State Government. If it is a private land, one has to preferably purchase on outright basis. While selecting the site for the project, the entrepreneur should ensure the following:

(i) Area should be accessible preferably by a road even during the monsoon season.

(ii) Mangrove area with large tree stumps should not be selected.

(iii) Site should have good pollution free water supply of both freshwater and brackish water. Water quality parameters required for maximum feed efficiency and maximum growth of *Penaeus monodon* are given below:

	Water Parameters	Optimum Level
1.	Dissolved Oxygen	3.5-4 ppm
2.	Salinity	10-25 ppt
3.	Water Temperature	26-32 (°C)
4.	pH	6.8-8.7
5.	Total nitrite nitrogen	1.0 ppm
6.	Total ammonia (less than)	1.0 ppm
7.	Biological Oxygen Demand (BOD)	10 ppm
8.	Chemical Oxygen Demand (COD)	70 ppm
9.	Transparency	35 cm
10.	Carbon dioxide (less than)	10 ppm
11.	Sulphide (less than)	0.003 ppm

(iv) The areas should be flood free.

(v) Location with a natural slope, for proper drainage should be selected.

(vi) Social problems due to competing use of water resources and drainage of waste water should be properly taken care of.

(vii) Availability of necessary infrastructure namely electricity, ice factory, cold storage, communication facilities etc., are necessary for successful management.

Borrowers' Profile

Complete details of the entrepreneurs, partnership firm, registered company should be given. Qualification and experience of the promoters, net worth of the borrowers, other activities undertaken by them, financial ability etc., have to be furnished.

Technical Feasibility of the Project

As the project envisaged new technologies, the borrowers may take the help of a competent outside agency to prepare the technical feasibility report on the project. However, the first and foremost requirement of the project is to get a licence from Aquaculture Authority as per the existing norms and as per guidelines issued by Supreme Court of India.

Physical and Financial Outlay

Details of the physical and financial outlays involved for setting up of 5 ha. Brackish water prawn farm are furnished in Annexure No.II. It can be seen therefrom that the total cost including working capital expenses for raising the first crop for a 5 ha. Prawn farm works out to Rs. 37.60 lakhs. While submitting the project to the banks for sanction of loan entrepreneurs are expected to submit detailed plan and estimates for all the civil works to be undertaken as also invoices of various items to be purchased from the suppliers.

Margin Money and Bank Loan

The entrepreneur has to bring in 25% of the project cost out of his own resources and the balance of 75% will be provided by banks as bank loan. However, NABARD could consider providing margin money loan assistance in suitable and eligible cases as per the guidelines contained in circular no. DPD 67/92-93 dated 24.2.1993.

Rate of Refinance

NABARD refinance is available for projects for setting up of shrimp farms provided the same is technically feasible and financially viable. NABARD is agreeable to provide refinance as per existing norms.

Financial Viability

For undertaking shrimp culture within CRZ and outside CRZ the following assumptions have been made which are shown in the table below:

	Improved Traditional (within CRZ)	Extensive (outside CRZ)	
(i)	Farm Size	5 ha	5 ha
(ii)	Culture period	4-4½ months	4-4 ½ months
(iii)	Stocking density (PL-20)	50,000/- ha	1,00,000/- ha
(iv)	Survival	70%	65%
(v)	Expected production	1.2 tonnes/ha/crop	2.5tonnes/ha corp
(vii)	Price of shrimp has been taken as Rs.250/kg		

The financial analysis for extensive system of shrimp farming has been shown in Annexure No. III. Results of the analysis are as under:

(i) NPW at 15% DF - Rs. 61.314 lakhs.

(ii) BCR at 15% DF - 1.515

(iii) IRR is more than 50 per cent

Marketing

Because of huge gap between supply and demand of shrimps in local as well as international market, there may not be any problem in marketing the same. Shrimps can either be sold directly by the farmers in the market or sold to exporters for processing before export. Shrimps can be exported in frozen form with head on , head less, battered and breaded, or IQF products or any other form with value addition. The prawn has to be packed as per requirements of importing countries and therefore this should be decided after a detailed market survey. It is always advisable to get in touch with local distributing agents of the customer country. Hygienic packaging, display and appearance of the packet are key factors to attract consumers of importing countries.

Rate of Interest

As per existing RBI guidelines interest rate to be charged to the ultimate borrower for loan exceeding Rs.2 lakhs will be as decided by the lending Bank. NABARD's interest rate for refinance would be as per existing norms prevailing at the particular time.

Repayment Period

It will be able to repay the bank loan in five years with a moratorium of one year on repayment of principal.

Security

Security from the ultimate beneficiaries has to be obtained as per the rules of financing banks which have to be in conformity with the guidelines of Reserve Bank of India.

Conclusion

As shrimps have got good export potential, establishment of shrimp farms as per the model scheme indicated above is recommended for consideration by banks for financing.

Technical Parameters for Establishing a Extensive Shrimp Farm

1. *Design and Construction of shrimp Farm*

An extensive shrimp farm should be of the size 0.4-0.5 ha and preferably drainable from the management point of view. The ponds generally should have concrete dikes, elevated concrete supply canal with separate drain gates and adequate life supporting devices like generators and aerators.

The design, elevation and orientation of the water canals must be related to the elevation of the area with particular reference to the mean range of tidal fluctuation. The layout of the canals and dikes may be fitted as closely as technically possible to existing land slopes and undulation for minimizing the cost of construction.

2. *General Earth Work*

It is normally carried out in the following order:

1. Site clearing
2. Top soil stripping
3. Staking of centre lines and templates
4. Preparation of dike foundation
5. Excavation of drainage canals
6. Construction of dikes (peripheral and secondary)
7. Forming and compaction of dikes.
8. Excavation of pits for gates.
9. Levelling of pond bottom.
10. Construction of gates and refilling of pits
11. Construction of dike protection.

The top soil may be set aside and should again be spread later to preserve pond bottom fertility.

3. *The Essential Components of a Shrimp farm are:*

1. Ponds
2. Water intake structure
3. Store room for feed and equipments
4. An area for cleaning of the harvest
5. A workshop and pump house
6. Watch and ward room, office and a mini laboratory.

4. *Ponds*

From the management point of view it is better to go in for ponds of 0.4 ha-0.5 ha size. These ponds should be preferably completely drainable. The ponds are partitioned by secondary dykes. In order to render over all protection to the cultured stock and all related structures a perimeter dyke also can be constructed.

The height of the perimeter dyke will depend upon the following factors, such as:

1. Height of water level in the area.
2. Elevation above mean sea level.
3. Height of free board.
4. The percentage allowance for soil shrinkage.

The partition dykes determine the size and limit of each grow out pond and its height is determined by the following factors namely:

1. The height of water column in the pond
2. Free board
3. Wave action
4. Shrinkage factor

The shrinkage factor is decided by the type of soil like heavy, medium and light soils.

Gates

They regulate the inflow and outflow of water into the pond and also are responsible for maintaining the desired water column in the pond. The main gates are constructed on the perimeter dyke and are usually located on the partition dykes and they regulate the water column in the individual ponds. It can be made out of concrete or PVC or Asbestos piping.

Drain Canals

They are generally trapezoidal in cross section and its discharge capability is decided by area of cross section and velocity of water flow.

Pond Preparation

Proper pond preparation will ensure higher production. The main objectives of pond preparation are:

1. To eradicate weed fishes and orgnaisms
2. To remove abnoxious gases
3. To improve the natural productivity of the pond eco system
4. To maintain high water quality for proper growth and higher survival percentage.

Eradication of unwanted organisms is usually carried out by draining out the entire water and drying the pond bottom till it cracks. This also helps in removal of obnoxious gases and oxygenation of the pond bottom. It also improves the fertility of the soil.

Liming is done for correcting the pH and to kill pathogenic bacteria and virus. In undrainable ponds mahual oil should be applied @ 200 ppm to eradicate the weed fishes. After around two weeks time organic and inforanic fertilisers are applied to enrich the soil and water. Once the thick lab-lab is formed the water level is raised and the pond is made ready for stocking.

Selective Stocking

The most suitable species for culture in India are the Indian white prawn Penaeus indicus and tiger prawn P. Monodon. The stocking density varies with the type of system adopted and the species selected for the culture. As per the directives of Supreme Court only traditional and improved traditional shrimp farming can be undertaken within the CRZ with a production range of 1 to 1.5 tonnes/ha/crop with stocking density of 40,000 to 60,000/ ha/crop. Outside CRZ extensive shrimp farming with a production range of 2.5 to 3 tonnes/ha/crop with stocking density of 1,00,000/ha/crop may be allowed.

In order to have uniform growth of the cultured animal it is always advisable to go in for hatchery reared seeds.

Food and Feeding

Shrimp diets may be supplementary or complete. In a extensive system the shrimps need a complete diet. Although natural food items have good conversion values but they are difficult to procure in large quantities and maintain a continuous supply.

At present most of the aquaculture farms depend on imported feed with a FCR of 1:1.5 - 1.8. The feeding could be done by using automatic feed dispensers, or by broadcasting all over the pond. If feeding trays are employed in selected pockets in the pond wastage in feed can be reduced.

HARVESTING

Complete harvesting can be carried out by draining the pond water through a bag net and hand picking. The average culture period required is around 120-150 days during which time the prawns will grow to 20-30 gm size (depending on the species). It is possible to get two crops in a year. Harvested shrimps can be kept between layers of crushed ice before transporting the consignment to market.

3

Endangerment of Marine Species

Introduction

When discussing the causes of endangerment, it is important to understand that individual species are not the only factors involved in this dilemma. Endangerment is a broad issue, one that involves the habitats and environments where species live and interact with one another. Although some measures are being taken to help specific cases of endangerment, the universal problem cannot be solved until humans protect the natural environments where endangered species dwell.

There are many reasons why a particular species may become endangered. Although these factors can be analyzed and grouped, there are many causes that appear repeatedly. Below are several factors leading to endangerment.

Habitat Destruction

Our planet is continually changing, causing habitats to be altered and modified. Natural changes tend to occur at a gradual pace, usually causing only a slight impact on individual species. However, when changes occur at a fast pace, there is little or no time for individual species to react and adjust to new circumstances. This can create disastrous results, and for this reason, rapid habitat loss is the primary cause of species endangerment. The strongest forces in rapid habitat loss are human beings. Nearly every region of the earth has been affected by human activity, particularly during this past century. The loss of microbes in soils that formerly supported tropical forests, the extinction of fish and various aquatic species in polluted habitats, and changes in global climate brought about by the release of greenhouse gases are all results of human activity.

It can be difficult for an individual to recognize the effects that humans have had on specific species. It is hard to identify or predict human effects on individual species and habitats, especially during a human lifetime. But it is quite apparent that human activity has greatly contributed to species endangerment. For example, although tropical forests may look as though they are lush, they are actually highly susceptible to destruction. This is because the soils in which they grow are lacking in nutrients. It may take centuries to re-grow a forest that was cut down by humans or destroyed by fire, and many of the world's severely threatened animals and plants live in these forests. If the current rate of forest loss continues, huge quantities of plant and animal species will disappear.

Introduction of Exotic Species

Native species are those plants and animals that are part of a specific geographic area, and have ordinarily been a part of that particular biological landscape for a lengthy period of time. They are well adapted to their local environment and are accustomed to the presence of other native species within the same general habitat. Exotic species, however, are interlopers. These species are introduced into new environments by way of human activities, either intentionally or accidentally. These interlopers are viewed by the native species as foreign elements. They may cause no obvious problems and may eventual be considered as natural as any native species in the habitat. However, exotic species may also seriously disrupt delicate ecological balances and may produce a plethora of unintended yet harmful consequences.

The worst of these unintended yet harmful consequences arise when introduced exotic species put native species in jeopardy by preying on them. This can alter the natural habitat and can cause a greater competition for food. Species have been biologically introduced to environments all over the world, and the most destructive effects have occurred on islands. Introduced insects, rats, pigs, cats, and other foreign species have actually caused the endangerment and extinction of hundreds of species during the past five centuries. Exotic species are certainly a factor leading to endangerment.

Overexploitation

A species that faces overexploitation is one that may become severely endangered or even extinct due to the rate in which the species is being used. Unrestricted whaling during the 20th century is an example of overexploitation, and the whaling industry brought many species of whales to extremely low population sizes. When several whale species were nearly extinct, a number of nations (including the United States) agreed to abide by an international moratorium on whaling. Due to this moratorium, some whale species, such as the grey whale, have made remarkable comebacks, while others remain threatened or endangered.

Due to the trade in animal parts, many species continue to suffer high rates of exploitation. Even today, there are demands for items such as rhino horns and tiger bones in several areas of Asia. It is here that there exists a strong market for traditional medicines made from these animal parts.

More Factors

Disease, pollution, and limited distribution are more factors that threaten various plant and animal species. If a species does not have the natural genetic protection against particular pathogens, an introduced disease can have severe effects on that specie. For example, rabies and canine distemper viruses are presently destroying carnivore populations in East Africa. Domestic animals often transmit the diseases that affect wild populations, demonstrating again how human activities lie at the root of most causes of endangerment. Pollution has seriously affected multiple terrestrial and aquatic species, and limited distributions are frequently a consequence of other threats;

populations confined to few small areas due to of habitat loss, for example, may be disastrously affected by random factors.

Aqua mats are a new and innovative aquaculture product fabricated from highly specialized synthetic substrates to produce supplemental organic food resource, primarily phytoplankton, zooplankton and bacteria. Aqua mats resemble sea grass in appearance and provide aquatic habitat, in situ biofiltration and supplemental natural food production for a wide range of aquatic species and environments. At the same time that Aqua mats generate a continuously replenished organic food supplement using natural biological processes, the product provides aquatic structure (to support higher stocking densities, reproduction and reduce predation) and effluent control for most aquatic species. Aqua mats products include aquaculture (rearing shrimp and fish species), ornamental ponds (for use in water gardening and koi ponds) and for use in recreational lakes and ponds.

Product Description

Surface Deployment Format (SDF) Aqua mats are suspended from the water surface and the individual ribbons are non buoyant, sink to the pond bottom and deploy into a complex three dimensional structure. Each surface of the ribbons is engineered with the Ultra weave TM process to promote growth of benthic organisms rich in highly bioavailable HUFA's, vitamin and minerals on one side and beneficial biofiltration organisms on the other. The upper section of SDF Aqua mats consists of a durable flotation element inserted in a highly UV resistant sleeve.(In this design wave energy is transmitted to the submerged bioactive surfaces, displacing sediment accumulation and assuring high levels of periphyton growth.) The upper layer of the SDF product promotes growth of benthic organisms rich in highly bioavailable HUFA's, vitamins and minerals. The lower Ultra weave layer promotes growth of beneficial biofiltration organisms and provides optimal shelter. The SDF Aqua mats feature easier unit deployment and retrieval, lower unit weight and detachable ballast bags. Models: 120002.00 for nursery and grow out.

What is Ultra Weave

Ultra weave is the name given to the revolutionary manufacturing technology that is used to microscopically tailor the surface construction of Aqua mats. The ultra weave TM process achieves optimal product performance for the entire line of Aqua mats products in ponds, and in commercial aquatic farming and in biofiltration applications.

How does Ultra Weave Technology Work

Ultra weave TM technology provides bioengineered, precision substrates to encourage the growth of select bacterial and benthic algal communities. The pore size and other key characteristics of the surfaces for each product within the product line are also tailored and specified to achieve the right balance between algal and bacterial community colonization for the specific product application. By its unique surface engineering, Ultra weave TM technology provides the optimal balance of natural feed production and supplemental biofiltration capacity.

Biofiltration Applications

Early product trials in aquaculture demonstrated that the bluegreen algae typically formed late in commercial growth cycles, did not develop in ponds with Aqua mats .This is because the soluble reactive phosphorus was very rapidly metabolized by the periphyton community on the surfaces of the Aqua mats. Moreover, the periphyton community generally tolerated a far wider ratio in total nitrogen/total phosphorus. The combined effect of these characteristics allowed the periphyton community supported on the surfaces of Aqua mats to dominate in utilization of available phosphorus and in the process out competes bluegreen algae available P resource. This phenomena has been used to advantage in guiding Meridian's Ultra weave technology in all of the Aqua mats products lines, especially in biofiltration applications.

Benefits in Crustaceans

Aqua mats have demonstrated the capability to remove as much as 82% of available phosphorus with hydraulic residence times of 24 hours or longer, as well as 90% of the nitrates in 36 hours. Ammonia is also rapidly removed by aerobic bacteriological nitrification process. The removal of these nutrients allows the stocking of even higher densities in ponds, tanks and raceways, while at the same time reducing the environmental impact of Aquaculture operations. Aqua mats have demonstrated tremendous value in culture of crustaceans, particularly penaeid shrimps. The primary benefits and functions of Aqua mats in shrimp are:

Zero Water Exchange System

- Provides structure that allows for at least a 50% to 100% increase in stocking density with no fall off in survival.
- Increase natural feed production substantially and reduce overall FCR values.

Improve Immune System Function.

- Controls soluble toxins and effluent discharge by performing insitu biofiltration.

Increase Dissolved Oxygen Levels without Aeration

Aqua mats provide vertical structure that dramatically increases the surface area available for grazing and reduces cannibalistic predation. Stocking levels as high as 160 animals per square meter in 1 meter deep tanks for penaeid shrimp have been achieved with very high survival rates. With adequate nutrients and sunlight, the regenerative periphyton on the surface of Aqua mats provides a very large proportion of the feed necessary during early rearing (45 or more days) of all crustacean species. Aqua mats continue to provide shrimp species with an important natural food supplement throughout their life cycle. In zero exchange aquaculture systems, as much as 92% of available nitrogen and 75% of phosphorus is converted to periphyton biomass. Phosphorus fixation rates range between 25 and 30 mg/sq m./day on Aqua mats .Nitrogen fixation rates range between 1.3 and 0.5 grams/day/sq.m/day. The Ultra weave technology used in manufacturing operations, generates an anaerobic zone only microns thick on one side of the product to enhance mass transfer and rapid denitrification while the other side of the product is manufactured with higher loft to generate more holdfast area for surface oriented algae species and bacteria. Aqua mats for biofiltration represent a highly unique and advantageous method of applying periphyton based processes into all dimensions of the water column in order to reduce excess nutrient loads.

Lakes/Nutrient Control and Habitat Applications

Aqua mats technology for use in ponds and lakes where the primary interest is in increasing the health of the ecosystem and the success of stocked or indigenous fish populations. Aqua mats for Lakes are factory configured for immediate out of the box lakeside installation to afford lake owners/managers with epilithon based natural algae control and habitat to increase the success of fish and many other species in the pond ecosystem. The epilithon based community that rapidly colonizes Aqua mats for lakes reduces water column nutrient levels dramatically as the Aqua mats supported epilithon community out competes the phytoplankton community in natural processes.

Ornamental Pond Applications

The aqua mats for ornamental ponds product provides pond owners with a revolutionary, in-pond biofiltration system that combines a pleasing plant-like appearance with bio-engineered surfaces that add vast amounts of beneficial biological activity to ornamental ponds and water gardens. The basic benefits that characterize and distinguish the product are as follows:

- Enhances complements and reduces the load on existing pond biofiltration systems.
- Provides valuable habitat for pond fish to play and seek shelter from the sun and from predators.
- Provides a "safety net" in the event of failure or interruption of mechanical pond systems.
- Biological growth on the Aqua mats surfaces provide fish with highly desirable natural food.

- Relief from excessive green water through natural biological processes.
- Eco-friendly construction using food grade polymers with no parts to replace, no power required and no recurring cost burden.
- Long lasting, low-cost, easy to handle and install.s

Installation

The SDF Aqua mats are simple to use and install either in dry or in already filled ponds. The top portion of SDF Aqua mats floats at the water surface. It maintains its relative position in the pond by ballast bags(supplied) that are attached to the lower sections of the product. For best results, it is recommended that SDF Aqua mats be installed 5-10 days prior to the introduction of Pl's in order to develop initial productivity while the pond is being filled and bloomed. Initial SDF Aqua mats productivity is dominated by benthic diatoms which are of great food value and highly utilized by PL's. SDF Aqua mats may also be installed during the early stages of the grow out cycle.

Aquatic Invasive Species

Thousands of freshwater, estuarine, and marine species have been dispersed or transplanted across the globe by humans. These aquatic invasive species arrive in the ballast or on the hulls of ships, through the movement of shellfish and bait, by the opening of new channels or canals, through intentional release, and other vectors. Once established, they can change ecosystems, reduce native biodiversity. and impact local economies. Aquatic communities are becoming increasingly homogenized as a result.

In recent years, the introduction rate of plants, animals, and protists and other microorganisms has been accelerating. The invasion rate of freshwater cladocera, small crustaceans such as the water flea *Daphnia,* is now 50,000 times higher than the background level before humans played a dominant role in species transport. In San Francisco Bay, a new aquatic species becomes established every 14 weeks. (Before 1960, the rate was approximately once every 55 weeks.) This acceleration is likely because of a rise in propagule pressure, the number of individuals released in a particular area, and human disturbance to aquatic systems. Propagule pressure has risen as a result of increased shipping traffic and aquacultural activities. Humans have also changed aquatic systems through eutrophication (the increase of nutrients such as nitrogen and phosphorus), the removal of top predators, and other modifications.

San Francisco Bay is one of the most invaded bodies of water and also one of the best studied. There are now over 230 exotic species in the bay, and in some communities, nonindigenous species make up more than 95% of the biomass and total abundance of organisms. New species have come in through ship fouling, ballast water, intentional transplants, or by hitchhiking along with bait packaging. Hydrozoans, amphipods, isopods, copepods, mollusks, crustaceans, and algae have all become established in the bay in recent decades. Surprisingly, the establishment of an introduced species, rather than impeding further invasions, appears to facilitate the settlement of other nonindigenous species. Interactions among species can accelerate the impacts to native ecosystems leading to an invasional meltdown.

San Francisco Bay is well studied, but not alone. From the Great Lakes to Tokyo Bay and the coast of Tasmania, species have been transported around the globe since humans first took to the seas. In fact, there are probably few if any marine, coastal, or inland water systems that have not been impacted by aquatic invasives. At least 70 alien species have been found in every estuary that has been surveyed in the continental US. The number is likely much higher, as many species may have been transported in ancient times before there was detailed information on aquatic flora and fauna.

Ballast Water and Other Vectors

Vector provides the means of transport from a species' native range to its new environment. Ships and boats have probably been the primary vectors for moving aquatic invasive species. Historically, organisms may have attached themselves to the hulls of vessels or been transported through dry ballast, such as rocks and sand. In recent years, ballast water has become a major vector. On any given day, thousands of species are transported around the world via ships. Post-transport ballast water contains high densities of both *holoplankton*, organisms such as dinoflagellates and jellyfish that spend their entire life as plankton, and *meroplankton*, the temporary larval stages of crustaceans, worms, and fish. Because ballast tanks may hold millions of liters of water, numerous individuals can be introduced in a single event.

The construction of canals can remove dispersal barriers, allowing species to cross between water systems that may have been isolated for millions of years. The completion of the Suez Canal in 1869, for example, led to the Mediterranean incursion of several species for the Red Sea. These Lessepsian migrants, named after Ferdinand de Lesseps, the French diplomat responsible for the construction of the canal, show no signs of reduced genetic diversity in their new range, indicating that individuals regularly cross the canal.

Many fish species, such as the Nile perch (*Lates niloticus*) in Lake Victoria and Asian swamp eels (*Monopterus albus*) in the US, have been intentionally released as food sources. Others like the walleye (*Stizostedion vitreum*) and rainbow trout (*Oncorhynchus mykiss*) have been moved to stock waterways for sport fishing. Additional important vectors include releases from aquariums, both intentional and accidental, and commercial aquaculture, especially shellfish. Oyster transfer is considered the primary vector for the spread of invasive macroalgae in the Mediterranean and is probably the source for many invasive animals as well. Algal packing material used for shipping live seafood and bait may contain juvenile crabs, snails, mussels, and other organisms. Often discarded near shore, live seaweed appears to be emerging as an important vector in the United States.

Ecological and Economic Consequences

This comb jelly, native to the western Atlantic, was introduced into the Black Sea in the 1980s and has spread to the Mediterranean and Caspian. The invasion caused a catastrophic decline in zooplankton and pelagic fisheries. The anchovy fishery in the region has had losses estimated in the hundreds of millions of US dollars per year. Fish and invertebrate diversity is at serious risk from this small but Aquatic invasions can lead to profound ecological changes. New species may be competitors, disturbers, consumers, or prey. They can cause local extinctions through competitive exclusion, niche displacement, hybridization and introgression with native species, and predation. The seaweeds *Caulerpa taxifolia* and *C. racemosa* overgrow seagrasses, creating monocultures that have been described as biological deserts. Filter feeders and species that act as ecosystem engineers, creating and modifying habitats, can have big impacts on biodiversity and ecosystem function. The Japanese eelgrass (*Zostera japonica*) for example, converts tidal flats, important foraging grounds for shorebirds, to eelgrass beds and alters nutrient fluxes in its invasive range in the Pacific Northwest.

A species' arrival may be spectacular, as in the case of zebra mussels (*Dreissena polymorpha*) in the Great Lakes or the comb jelly *Mnemiopsis leidyi* in Europe, or it may go unnoticed in the absence of molecular tools and careful monitoring. Along the coast of California, the decline of the native bay mussel, *Mytilus trossulus,* was undetected until genetic assays revealed that a nonnative species, *M. galloprovincialis,* had displaced it from much of its range. The two species now exist in a highly dynamic state, following temperature and salinity gradients in a pattern that includes hybrid zones. After several aquacultural introductions, all three species of blue mussels (*M. galloprovincialis, M. trossulus,* and *M. edulis*) have now hybridized in Puget Sound in the Pacific Northwest of the United States.

Human-mediated invasions cost billions of dollars in damages each year, impacting commercial and recreational fisheries, ecosystem services, human health, and native biodiversity. One study estimates the impact of all invasive species, including terrestrial and microbial species, as more than $314 billion per year for six countries (U.S., U.K., Australia, South Africa, India, and Brazil). In the US, environmental losses from invasive mussels are $1.3 billion per year, and $1 billion per year for invading fish. After *Mnemiopsis* became established in the Black Sea, the collapse of the anchovy fishery cost harvesters about $250 million per year.

Invasions cause ecological change, but human alteration of the environment can also facilitate the establishment of nonnative species. Overfishing, habitat destruction, climate change, eutrophication, and pollution can alter aquatic ecosystems, making them more vulnerable to invasion. Wastewater discharge and bottom trawling in the Mediterranean impacted native seagrasses, helping an invasive strain of the tropical algae *Caulerpa taxifolia* colonize more than 130 square kilometers of seafloor in six countries in less than 20 years. Rapid expansion of the algal clone continues. In the Gulf of Maine, climate change and sustained overfishing may be acting synergistically, creating an environment that favors invasive species such as the green alga *Codium fragile* and the bryozoan *Membranipora membranacea*.

Genetics of Invasions

The green crab (*Carcinus maenas*) is native to Europe and North Africa. It has a well-established invasion record, spanning two centuries and five continents. The earliest is from eastern North America in 1817, then Australia in 1900. In recent years, this global invader has appeared in Tasmania, South Africa, Japan, western North America, and Argentina.

The traditional scenario of a biological invasion is a single successful inoculation and colonization event, followed by the establishment of a self-sustaining population and spread of the species. The startling rise in the success of aquatic invasive species has occurred despite this apparent 'genetic paradox.' Small founding populations of introduced species are expected to have genetic variation that is lower than that of native populations as a result of bottlenecks. Lessons learned from conservation genetics lead us to expect that such arrivals would be subject to high risk of inbreeding and extinction. Drift and founder events should also limit the ability of such populations to adapt. How then do these species become established, expand their invasive range and respond to novel environmental conditions? In many cases, introduced species don't have to overcome these effects. The discharge from the ballast of a large ship can release numerous individuals in a single event. Preliminary bottlenecks can be overcome by gene flow from multiple source populations, a pattern that has been found in the European green crab (*Carcinus maenas*) in North America, the Eurasian spiny waterflea in the Great Lakes, and numerous species that have undergone genetic analysis. Genetic variation is not essential for invasion success. Some species invade as clones. A single American lineage of *D. pulex* replaced a diverse assemblage of genotypes in Africa. In 75 years, this new lineage has become dominant despite the presence of resting native egg banks and competition from native *D. pulex* and ten additional daphnid species.

Beyond the ability to determine variation and infer propagule pressure, genetic tools can be used to detect, identify, and monitor invasive species. Because morphological identification of larvae and eggs can be particularly challenging, genetic techniques such as DNA barcoding, which employs variation in DNA sequences to identify particular taxa, offer promise to help uncover cryptic invasions. Molecular studies may also prove helpful in the postinvasion control of aquatic introduction. An understanding of genetics will be critical in assessing proposed control efforts of introduced species using genetic engineering or parasites and pathogens.

Management

The prevention of invasions requires the management of vectors from the point of origin to arrival. Effective quarantine regulations are essential. More than 50 national and international laws and regulations are in place to restrict the transport of nonnative species. Yet few of these carry stiff penalties for noncompliance. To date, Australia and New Zealand have some of the most proactive approaches to preventing, eradicating, and controlling aquatic invasive species.

Ballast-water exchange is generally considered to be one of the most effective ways to reduce the number of potential propagules crossing the oceans. In the United States, the highly publicized spread of the zebra mussel in the Great Lakes in 1988 helped pass the Non-indigenous Aquatic Nuisance Prevention and Control Act of 1990. The law was expanded and renamed the National Invasive Species Act, or NISA, in 1996. Ships entering the Great Lakes are now required to exchange their freshwater ballast with salt water before entering the lakes. Yet for many coastal areas, ballast-water exchange remains voluntary and the efficacy of the programme unknown.

Government policy to prevent new species introductions is more cost effective than control after establishment. In addition to ballast-water exchange, fouling management programs have been proposed to help reduce the spread of organisms from communities that foul the hulls of ships. Public education about the risks of releasing aquatic plants and pets and the accidental distribution of exotics in bait and seafood algal packaging materials is also essential in curbing the damage from these vectors.

Once an aquatic invasive species has been established, physical removal has rarely been successful. More than 30,000 Northern Pacific seastars (*Asterias amurensis*) were removed from the shallow waters of southern Tasmania in 1993. In 2001, there were more than 140 million individuals in the area. Yet there are a few success stories. About 1,600,000 native turban snails (*Tegula funebralis*) were taken by hand from the rocky intertidal zone of southern California to prevent the spread of an introduced South African worm that infected the mollusks. No infections were detected after the snails were removed and screens were installed at the suspected source, an abalone aquacultural facility.

Eradication is less costly than prolonged control programs, and it is most feasible in the early stages of invasion when distribution is limited. Risk assessments, including the probability that a species will establish and the harm that it is likely to cause, can be used to prioritize management actions. Introduced species that can facilitate later invasions are of special concern. The arrival of the European green crab in San Francisco Bay, for example, resulted in the aggressive spread of a previously rare introduced bivalve in the western US.

In some cases, biocontrol is a possibility. The use of parasites, species-specific predators, or disease can help reduce the impact of invasive species in freshwater and marine ecosystems, although there are risks involved with introducing new species into ecosystems. The development of new fisheries has been proposed to reduce populations of edible invasives, such as the European green crab and common periwinkle (*Littorina littorea*) in northeastern North America, although cultural barriers and concerns about creating a sustainable market for the exotics remain.

Mukellunge Distribution and Identification

The muskie, a member of the pike family (Esocidae), is a top predator in freshwaters of the Great Lakes region. The natural range of the muskie spans from north to south from Tennessee to mid-Ontario, and from east to west from New York to Minnesota. Muskie can reach lengths of over 50 inches and weights of over 50 pounds. Their appearance is streamlined, with their dorsal fin located directly above the anal fin, and their mouth is equipped with sharp canine teeth. Muskie generally fall into one of, or a combination of, three distinct color phases: spotted, barred, or clear.

Muskie from the upper Mississippi watershed and Great Lakes, including Lake St. Clair, are generally spotted, with most inland muskie in the Midwestern United States falling into the barred or clear phases. As with most species, though, color and markings are not the best way to identify the muskellunge. Northern pike (*Esox lucius*) is a closely related species in the pike family that reaches similar sizes as muskie, and could easily be confused with muskellunge. To distinguish between northern pike and muskie, the head must be closely examined. Muskellunge have six or more pores on the underside of their jaws and the upper half of their cheeks are scaled, while northern pike have 5 or fewer pores and entirely scaled cheeks. A final anatomical feature to check is the tail, with muskie tails being more deeply forked and northern pike tails being more rounded off. Hybridization between muskie and northern pike is possible, with the resultant tiger muskellunge displaying characteristics of both parents. Tiger muskie generally have both bars and spots, making it appear more like a muskie than a northern pike, but the tiger muskie tail is usually rounded like the northern pike (Figure 1). For more thorough anatomical descriptions see Trautman (1981).

Muskie, northern pike, and tiger muskie identification. Artist- Virgil Beck, for more information visit the Trent University web Unlike many coolwater, freshwater species it is possible to visually determine the sex of mature muskellunge. In adult female muskie the urogenital region resembles the shape of a pear, while in adult male muskellunge the shape of the region resembles a keyhole. Sexually dimorphic growth occurs with muskellunge, as females reach larger ultimate sizes than males. Another interesting fact about the muskellunge is that there is evidence that muskie have a different sex-determining system than northern pike. While northern pike appear to use an XY system similar to ours (with males being XY and females being XX), uncovered evidence of a WZ system (with males being ZZ and females being WZ) in muskellunge. Simply stated, in northern pike, males determine the sex of offspring, while in muskie, females determine the sex of offspring.

Mukellunge Biology

Muskellunge and northern pike many times inhabit similar habitats, and research in Minnesota revealed a few interesting findings. Muskie, in the absence of northern pike, tend to reproduce in the same shallow, weedy areas that would normally be dominated by northern pike spawning during the spring. However, in the presence of northern pike the muskellunge tend to spawn in slightly deeper water, yielding the more preferred habitat to the northern pike. The presence or absence of northern pike also appears to impact ultimate growth of muskellunge. Muskie inhabiting waters without northern pike rarely reach total lengths of more than 40 inches, while muskie in the presence of northern pike occasionally surpass 60 inches Muskie spawning generally occurs when water temperatures are in the 50's (°F), and a 40 pound female can produce about 200,000 eggs. Muskie larvae eat plankton after absorption of their yolk sac, and soon switch to a diet of strictly fish. Peak feeding periods for muskellunge usually occur when water temperatures are in the mid-60's.

Muskie Management

The large size and unpredictable nature of muskie have caused their popularity to grow with anglers in recent years. Muskie can reach speeds of near 30 miles per hour in short bursts, but have also earned the reputation of being the fish of "10,000 casts". Because of their popularity, intensive muskie management programs exist throughout the Midwest and Canada. In Ohio, for example, all inland muskie populations are maintained through yearly stockings of fingerlings. About 10 reservoirs are stocked on an annual basis with fingerlings ranging in size from 8 inches to 13 inches. Such intensive management is crucial due to the lack of spawning habitat in the man-made reservoirs of Ohio. Each spring adult muskellunge are netted from Clear Fork Reservoir by the Ohio Division of Wildlife for collection of eggs and sperm. The resulting larvae are then reared in state hatchery ponds for subsequent stocking. In Ohio, stocking densities of fingerlings usually range from 1 to 2 fish per acre, per year in selected reservoirs. Although intensive management strategies were important in creating and maintaining muskie fishing, the efforts would not have succeeded without the cooperation of anglers. A catch-and-release ethic has developed among muskie anglers, and has resulted in a return rate of more than 90% of caught muskellunge (personal communication, Richard Day, Ohio Division of Wildlife). The muskellunge has developed into a very popular sport fish, and intensive management combined with catch-and-release angling and responsible watershed management will maintain populations for years to come.

Paddlefish Interesting Facts

- In 1997 Missouri designated the paddlefish as the state's official aquatic animal.
- The paddlefish is the only species of family Polyodontidae in North America.
- Paddlefish eggs, or roe, are a popular caviar.
- Because they are filter-feeding planktivores, paddlefish cannot be caught by conventional fishing techniques. In states where it is legal, snagging has become a popular method of catching paddlefish.

- Paddlefish are a long-lived fish, surviving over 30 years in some cases. They also mature later than most fish, sometimes at 10 years or older.
- Paddlefish can attain sizes of over 7 feet long and more than 200 pounds.

Paddlefish Distribution and Identification

In Ohio, paddlefish are native to Lake Erie and the Ohio River and its tributaries. Although population densities have declined, paddlefish can still be found in the Ohio River and some of the major tributaries. Paddlefish have a very distinctive appearance, with the presence of a long snout, deeply forked tail, and are gray in color. The paddlefish's genus name, *Polyodon*, comes from a Greek word meaning "many tooth", and refers to their gill rakers . Their extensive gill rakers are used for filter feeding. Although paddlefish can reach large sizes (over 100 pounds), they feed primarily on plankton. The paddlefish's species name, *spathula*, is derived from a Latin word meaning "spatula" or "blade".

Paddlefish Biology

The function of the paddlefish's unique rostrum (paddle) has long been debated. Lon Wilkens, at the University of Missouri, St. Louis, conducted research that documented how the paddle functions. With the paddlefish reaching such large sizes, it is obvious that it must be very efficient at capturing mass amounts of food. Being primarily a river dweller, the paddlefish lives in a murky, harsh environment. Paddlefish are known to have poor eye sight, so to thrive in river environments their other senses must be extraordinary. The results of Lon Wilkens' research shows that paddlefish most likely use their long snout to detect prey.

Paddlefish feed on plankton, such as the water flea (*Daphnia*), that have been found to emit weak electrical signals. It appears as though the rostrum is a highly developed electro-receptor that can detect signals of less than 1/100th of one 1-millionth volt per centimeter. Laboratory studies verified that juvenile paddlefish will strike at electrodes placed in the water that emit currents similar to currents emitted by plankton. The response was verified by conducting the experiments in the dark, proving that the strike was not visually triggered. It was concluded that the paddlefish's rostrum is a highly sensitive "antenna" that aids the fish in not only feeding, but also navigation. When metal objects were place in the swim path of paddlefish, they routinely avoided them. However, when plastic objects were placed in their path, they usually collided with them.

Saugeye: Interesting Facts

- Saugeye are a hybrid created by crossing a female walleye with a male sauger
- Saugeye are a member of the perch family (Percidae)
- The Ohio state record saugeye weighed 12.84 pounds and was caught at Alum Creek Reservoir near Columbus
- Saugeye are stocked by a handful of states around the Midwest to create angling opportunities
- Saugeye eat mostly gizzard shad, shiners and yellow perch in Ohio reservoirs

Saugeye Distribution and Identification

Saugeye are a naturally occurring hybrid in water bodies that have reproducing populations of both walleye and sauger. It is suggested that in water bodies with walleye and sauger a hybridization rate of about 2-3% could be expected. It is found that 4.1% of all *Stizostedion* (walleye, sauger and saugeye) sampled in the Illinois river were saugeye. The sites sampled in the study had not been stocked and were sustained through natural reproduction.

In the 1980's state DNR's around the Midwest began experimenting with stocking saugeye as a sportfish in reservoirs and rivers. Throughout the 1960's and 70's walleye were stocked with little success in turbid, structure deficient reservoirs. In the late 70s it was discovered that saugeye not only survive better than walleye in reservoir habitats, they also grow faster and are more easily caught by anglers. Most likely a phenomenon known as "hybrid vigour" can explain the hybrid saugeye's aggressive feeding behaviors. Saugeye were immediately popular with anglers, and state's such as Ohio began replacing walleye with yearly stockings of saugeye.

Saugeye look similar to both parental species. Saugeye are best identified by their "blotchy" saddle markings on their side and back similar to sauger, but saugeye usually have white pigment on the lower portion of their tail along with dark blotches on their dorsal fin membrane. Identification of saugeye can be difficult in water bodies that have all three *Stizostedion* species, such as the Ohio River, but if it is possible to directly compare the three species at one time identification is much easier. Ohio, along with most other states that stock saugeye, does not stock both saugeye and walleye in any reservoir. To find out which species is stocked in your favorite water body check with your local DNR office.

Saugeye Biology

There is little doubt that saugeye stockings in reservoirs provide for better sportfishing than walleye stockings. Most reservoir systems lack the necessary water clarity and habitat required to support self-sustaining walleye populations. Stocking programs tend to be very costly when the time and effort needed to produce, raise and stock fingerlings is taken into consideration. When it became apparent that the sportfishing return was marginal for certain reservoirs stocked with walleye, stocking saugeye became an attractive option. Saugeye provided many benefits when compared to walleye. Saugeye generally are easier to rear than walleye, and as mentioned earlier, survive and grow better in reservoir systems. When creel surveys proved that saugeye were also easier to catch it seemed that stocking saugeye was the solution to provide better angling.

As early as the mid-1980s biologists began to notice an unexpected consequence of the saugeye stocking programs. It was originally assumed that saugeye would be sterile, because they are a hybrid species. Unfortunately, research projects started clearly documenting not only saugeye X walleye reproduction, but also saugeye X saugeye reproduction. Johnson et al. (1988) found that male saugeye crossed with female walleye resulted in 10% hatching success of second-generation hybrids. The walleye X saugeye not only documented reproduction, but also found saugeye X saugeye reproduction in Normandy Reservoir, Tamil Nadu (India).

Considering all of the potential genetic impacts associated with stocking saugeye, why do some states continue to stock them? For saugeye to have any impact on native populations of walleye and sauger, they must come into contact with them. By considering factors such as connectivity with other watersheds and presence of walleye and sauger, it is still possible to create great saugeye fisheries in situations where the risk for reproduction with parental species is low. For example, in Ohio, upground reservoirs and central Ohio reservoirs are stocked heavily with saugeye, but realistically those fish will never come into contact with native fish. The upground reservoirs are completely isolated from their water source, and central Ohio reservoirs are over 100 km from the Ohio River in most cases. While anglers stocking saugeye that they caught into other water bodies is always a risk, by cautiously selecting waters for yearly stockings state DNR's can create saugeye fishing opportunities without harming native fish populations.

Yellow Perch Interesting Facts

- Yellow perch are a member of the perch family (Percidae).
- Yellow perch spawning is very unique, they lay their eggs in long connected ribbons.
- Yellow perch can reach a maximum length of about 16" and weigh over 2 pounds.
- The Ohio state record yellow perch weighed 2.75 pounds and was caught on Lake Erie.
- Adult yellow perch diets are composed of small fish and invertebrates, such as mayfly larvae.

Distribution and Identification

Yellow perch are native to the upper Midwest and Canada, and usually have yellowish sides with dark vertical bars on their side and a white underside. They have sharp spines in their first dorsal fin, and during spawning their fins sometimes turn bright orange.

The yellow perch physiology has been a popular topic for research. Demand has increased for yellow perch as a food fish, and current commercial fisheries are not fulfilling the need. To increase the availability of yellow perch fillets, aquaculture researchers are documenting optimal conditions for culture of the species.

Great Lake's yellow perch populations (especially Lake Michigan) seem to be at a turning point. Exotic species introductions and other ecosystem changes appear to be negatively impacting yellow perch around the region. New research initiatives have been developed to better understand the problem, and state DNR management strategies have been developed to counteract the decreasing populations.

4

Aquatic Nuisance Species

Introduction

Aquatic Nuisance Species (ANS) are non-indigenous species that threaten the diversity or abundance of native species or the ecological stability of infested waters, or commercial, agricultural, aquacultural or recreational activities dependent on such waters. The ANS include nonindigenous species that may occur in inland, estuarine and marine waters and that presently or potentially threaten ecological processes and natural resources. In addition to adversely affecting activities dependant on waters of the United States, ANS adversely affect individuals, including health effects.

Nonindigenous Species (NIS) are any species or other viable biological material that enters an ecosystem beyond its historic range, including any such organism transferred from one country into another. Nonindigenous species include both exotics and transplants. Synonyms for NIS include *introduced, foreign, exotic, alien, non-native, immigrant* and *transplants*.

The table below provides a list of the three classes of adverse impacts caused by aquatic nuisance species:

Environmental Effects	*Economic Impacts*
Public Health	Predation
Industrial Water Users	Cholera Risk

Parasitism	Municipal Water Supplies
Competition	Nuclear Power Plants
Introduction of new pathogens	Commercial Fisheries
Genetic	Recreational Fishing
Habitat Alterations	Other Water Sports

Non-indigenous aquatic species impact biological and economic resources and can also impact human health. Nonindigenous species disturb native species through predation or displacement, clog intake pipes for municipal and industrial water supplies and can pose serious human health risks. Great Lakes water users spend tens of millions of dollars on zebra mussel control every year. Affected municipalities and industries, using large volumes of Great Lakes water, expend approximately $360,000 per year on zebra mussel control; small municipalities average $20,000. Nuclear power plants average an additional $825,000 of additional costs per year for zebra mussel control. As the zebra mussel spreads to inland lakes and rivers across North America, such as the Mississippi River Basin and Lake Champlain, so do the costs to water users. Other invading species of fish (such as the sea lamprey, ruffe and round goby) can harm native fish. Reductions in native fish populations (such as lake trout, walleye, yellow perch and catfish) threaten a sport and commercial fishing industry that is valued at almost $4.5 billion annually and supports 81,000 jobs.

Zebra mussel infestations cause pronounced ecological changes in the Great Lakes and major rivers of the central United States. The zebra mussel's rapid reproduction, coupled with consumption of microscopic plants and animals, affects the aquatic food web and places valuable commercial and sport fisheries at risk. In waters infested with the zebra mussel, large blooms of potentially toxic blue-green algae have been observed in waters such as Saginaw Bay, Lake Huron and the western basin of Lake Erie.

Non-indigenous aquatic nuisance plants, such as giant salvinia, purple loosestrife, Eurasian watermilfoil and hydrilla quickly establish themselves replacing native plants. Environmental and economic problems caused by the dense growth of these weeds include impairment of water-based recreation, navigation and flood control, degradation of water quality and fish and wildlife habitat, accelerated filling of lakes and reservoirs and depressed property values.

The ANS invasions also can pose serious health risks. A South American strain of human cholera bacteria was found in ballast tanks in the port of Mobile, Alabama in 1991. Cholera strains were also found in oyster and fin-fish samples in Mobile Bay, resulting in a public health advisory to avoid handling or eating raw oysters or seafood.

Every year, the introduction of harmful, non-native species into the U.S. has been increasing. Collectively, these nuisance species make tremendous impacts to different things valued by many Americans. Ultimately, the cost of invasive species (terrestrial and aquatic) in the United States amounts to more than $100 billion each year.

Reduce Game Fish Populations

One of the most significant impacts of Aquatic Hitchhikers is on game fish populations. Game fish have been impacted in numerous ways.

- **Directly killed by nuisance species.** Some nuisance species such as sea lamprey and whirling disease kill game fish directly:
  - Sea lampreys were discovered in Lake Michigan because of their impacts on Lake Trout. In fact, until fisheries biologists experimented with various control measures, the entire Lake Trout population was on the verge of crashing due to the sea lamprey invasion. Today, Canada and the U.S. governments collaborate to maintain an upper hand in the battle with the sea lamprey. Under the leadership of the Great Lakes Fisheries Commission, a bi-national approach spends approximately $14 million to combat sea lamprey.

- Whirling Disease is the result of a non-native parasite that attaches itself to trout and salmon. The parasite penetrates the head and spinal cartilage and causes the fish to swim erratically (whirl) and have difficulty feeding and avoiding predators. Because the fish cannot feed properly it eventually dies.

- **Through reduction of their food sources:** Species such as the zebra mussel, mudsnails, and round goby impact the food chain for native fish. In areas where gobies have become established, fishery managers have found substantial reductions in local populations of sculpins and darters which then impact the food chain of fish such as smallmouth bass and walleye. Zebra mussels disrupt the food chain by removing significant amounts of phytoplankton from the water, which are in turn food for larval and juvenile fish, which are in turn food for sport and commercial fisheries.

- **Negatively impacting reproduction:** Non-native species such as the common carp can make waters so turbid that eggs of native fish cannot survive. Others such as the round goby will feed on the eggs and fry of game fish. Nuisance plants, such as purple loosestrife, take over wetlands and eliminate native plants animals depend on for shelter and nesting.

- **Reducing oxygen content.** Nuisance plants such as water hyacinth and hydrilla reduce oxygen levels in the water putting stress on fish certain times of the year as well as actually causing fish kills due to lack of oxygen.

Ruin Boat Engines and Jam Steering Equipment

Other significant impact of Aquatic Hitchhikers is the effect on recreational boats. Non-native plants such as hydrilla and water hyacinth can clog water intakes on motors and thereby overheat and ruin your engine. Zebra mussels can also clog water intakes and have the potential to attach themselves to the prop and all areas of the motor, thereby either affecting the performance of the engine and or actually jamming steering equipment.

Make Lakes and Rivers Unusable by Boaters and Swimmers

Some harmful, non-native species, particularly plants like hydrilla and water hyacinth are so detrimental that they completely cover the waters they invade. Waters become so choked with these non-native plants that it is practically impossible to get a boat through and there is no open water left for swimmers to enjoy. Other nuisance species such as zebra mussels leave sharp-edged shells along swimming beaches which can be a hazard to unprotected feet.

Dramatically Increase the Operating Costs of Drinking Water Plants, Power Plants, Dam maintenance, and Industrial Processes

Industrial water users and businesses such as public utilities, power plants, municipal drinking water facilities and manufacturing industries all need a constant supply of water. However, with the proliferation of these harmful, non-native species like zebra mussels, many industries have had to develop costly control methods to maintain their water intake systems. The costs incurred from these control methods are eventually passed onto consumers, like you and me.

The Great Lakes provides a good example of the extent of aquatic nuisance species impacts. Water users in the region spend tens of millions of dollars on zebra mussel control every year. The zebra mussel attaches to hard surfaces and colonize on structures like those used for power and municipal water treatment plants. These industrial plants have reported significant reductions in pumping capabilities and occasional shutdowns.

- Affected municipalities and industries, using large volumes of Great Lakes water, have spent approximately $360,000 per year on zebra mussel control:
  - Small municipalities averaged $20,000 per year on control efforts.
  - Nuclear power plants averaged an additional $825,000 of additional costs per year for zebra mussel control.

The bottom line is that as zebra mussels and other aquatic hitchhikers spread to inland lakes and rivers across North America, like the Mississippi River Basin and Lake Champlain, so do the costs to water users.

Reduce Native Species

Invasive species impact nearly half of the species currently listed as Threatened or Endangered under the U.S. Federal Endangered Species Act. The section above on game fish covers how the native fish species are affected, but native plants and wildlife that live around the waters are also affected.

Harmful, non-native aquatic plants such as purple loosestrife, Eurasian watermilfoil and hydrilla quickly establish themselves replacing native plants. In addition to diminishing our nation's biological diversity by eliminating native species, the plants cause other serious environmental and economic problems.

In our natural world, everything is connected to everything else. When one aspect of an ecosystem is affected, it creates a domino affect resulting in many unforeseen changes. Zebra mussels provide a good example of how aquatic hitchhikers can cause pronounced ecological changes. In the Great Lakes, the zebra mussel's rapid reproduction, coupled with its consumption of microscopic plants and animals, has affected the fragility of this system's entire aquatic food web.

The impacts of rusty crayfish are another good examples. They reduce aquatic plant abundance and species diversity. Submerged native aquatic plants are important habitat for invertebrates (which provide food for fish and ducks), shelter for young game fish or forage species of fish, and nesting areas for fish. Also once native vegetation disappears, erosion can take place (plants minimize impact of waves) further adding to the degradation of an ecosystem.

Nuisance plant invasions trigger several domino affects. Water hyacinth is an example of a nuisance plant that degrades water quality by blocking photosynthesis, which greatly reduces oxygen levels in the water. This creates a cascading effect by reducing other underwater life such as fish and other plants. Water hyacinth also reduces biological diversity, impacts native submersed plants, alter immersed plant communities by pushing away and crushing them, and also alter animal communities by blocking access to the water and/or eliminating plants the animals depend on for shelter and nesting.

Another nuisance plant, purple loosestrife has taken over numerous wetlands. This harmful non-native plant has crowded out native vegetation and has impacted migratory birds. As a result waterfowl hunting and bird watching opportunities have diminished in areas affected by this plant.

The common carp is an example of a nuisance fish that has made a significant impact. It feeds by browsing on submerged vegetation - uprooting plants on which ducks feed, muddying the waters and destroying food and cover needed by other fish.

As significant filter feeders, zebra mussels may increase human and wildlife exposure to organic pollutants such as PCB's and PAHs. Early research shows that zebra mussels can rapidly accumulate organic pollutants within their tissues to levels more than 300,000 times greater than concentrations in the environment. They also deposit these pollutants in their pseudofeces. These contaminants can be passed up the food chain so that any fish or waterfowl consuming zebra mussels will also accumulate these organic pollutants. Likewise, human consumption of these same fish and waterfowl could result in further risk of exposure.

Other ANS invasions have been shown to pose additional health risks. A South American strain of human cholera bacteria was found in ballast tanks in the port of Mobile, Alabama in 1991. Cholera strains were also found in oyster and fin-fish samples in Mobile Bay, resulting in a public health advisory to avoid handling or eating raw oysters or seafood.

Reduce Property Values

Homes or lots adjacent to a quality water body (stream, lake, and coastal area) are valued substantially higher than those even a block away from the water. However, these waterfront values can quickly decline due to water quality problems. For example, in a community in Pennsylvania, two lakes set side by side, separated only by a small land mass. However, one lake is not able to support fish. The property value of homes on the fishless lake is lower than homes located a block away on the quality fishing lake. When lakes are choked with weeds where no recreation can occur, the property value is further reduced.

Impact Local Economies of Water-dependent Communities

Our country's economy is intimately linked to the health of our aquatic resources. The outdoor recreation industry derives significant benefits from dynamic aquatic systems, particularly mom-and-pop operations. However, this is only one of the many sectors that rely on the health of our waters for their economic viability. Throughout the country, coastal towns and cities have developed along our large river systems, the Great Lakes and the shores of the Gulf, the Atlantic and the Pacific. Collectively, these waters create a vast transportation network that facilitates commerce and ultimately provide the economic life blood that supports water-dependentcommunities.

So, when hitchhikers like the sea lamprey, ruffe or round goby enter into the waters where these coastal gateway communities are situated, much is at stake. Jobs and dollars are only the tip of the iceberg. In addition to the potential for significant, long-term ecological harm, lifestyles and entire family generations can be impacted by harmful, non-native species.

Put very simply, algae are a greenish/brownish growth that forms along the walls of your aquarium, or on plants and aquarium decorations. Algae are mostly chlorophyll producing photosynthetic organisms that resemble plants a lot. Contrary to plants, algae are single celled and are therefore not really plants. Excessive algae growth can be very frustrating for aquarists, especially for beginner aquarists and for those that have recently installed stronger lights. Since fish provide enough food for plants to grow, the chlorophyll filled algae too find your aquarium a safe breeding ground. Algae look ugly, and are difficult to eradicate completely. A small amount of algae is a natural part of the ecosystem and can even be an appreciated food source for many fish species. Once a thick carpet of algae forms in your aquarium, they will however begin to compete viciously for all the nutrients that your aquarium can provide. The "Algae Bloom" plagues almost every aquarium at one time or the other. Algae grow fast, especially when there is a regular supply of warm sunlight and rich nutrients.

Before we start off, it is necessary to know some inevitable facts about the relationship of an aquarium with algae. If you have an aquarium, then algae are inevitable. Algae can even be beneficial. When nutrient levels are very high in your aquarium, the algae consume the extra nutrients, thus making the water healthier for your fish. Algae also indicate that the ecosystem within your aquarium is healthy. Do not resort to chemical controlling of algae if you can get by with the natural method. If you try to chase away your algae too regularly, you will be causing too much of stress for your fish.

Here are several types of algae. The main categories include:

- The Green Algae;
- The Blue-Green; Algae
- The Red Algae; and
- The Diatoms.

The filamentous green algae form long green threads. These need abundant sunlight to flourish. They can be very damaging to plants as they rob them of vital nutrients. Filamentous green algae can be controlled by algae-eaters or by physical removal.

The suspended green algae look like green water. Large and frequent water changes will help to get rid of these. It will sometimes be necessary to use algaecides. The green spot algae form round spots on leaves and on the glass. Snails and algae eating fish can be used to remove these.

The blue-green algae are much more harmful than the green algae types and produce substances that are toxic for fish. Excessive illumination and high nitrate and phosphate levels create an ideal environment for these algae. Fish do not eat blue-green algae and the best way to get rid of these algae is a week of total darkness in the aquarium. Several water changes are also a must to get rid of them.

Diatoms form a layer of a brownish slime like substance on rocks, glass and plants. They are quickly eaten off by algae-eaters. They also subside when lighting intensity goes up.

Since Algae are unsightly and parasitic, it is necessary to keep their count low. There are some things that you can do to hamper the growth and spread of algae. The first and most important step is REGULAR water changes. Nothing can help you more than this. Remember, the reason you do not find algae floating in running streams is because the water in the streams keep changing at least a hundred times a day. Excess algae growth will instead be found in pools and puddles where the water is still. We can simulate nature very poorly when we change 20% of the water twice in a week. Change a little of your water as often as you can, and much of your algae problems will be solved.

At least once a month, take a special kind of aquarium scrubber and clean the glass of your aquarium completely. Some rocks contain certain minerals that will cause algae to grow rapidly. If you feel this could be the reason, remove the rocks immediately. Most algae need lots of sunlight. Keeping sunlight levels down, and using fluorescent lighting most of the time is also a simple way to keep the algae growth to a minimum.

New plants that come into your aquarium need to be treated to prevent algae from entering your aquarium. You can use Potassium Permanganate or Alum to treat your new plants. After soaking the plants in this for about 10 minutes, they should be rinsed thoroughly and then planted. Also remember to remove any weights or ties around the plants that you brought home. You should clean the fake plants or decorations in your aquarium by soaking them in a 1:20 solution of bleach to water for a few hours. These then need to be soaked in dechlorinated water. If you will be emptying out the entire contents of your aquarium, it is a good idea to soak your entire aquarium in fresh water with a dechlorinator.

Using algae-eating fish species and grazing snails will greatly help to keep down the amount of algae in your aquarium. As mentioned earlier, introducing algae-eaters as the first fish in your aquarium will greatly help to keep the algal growth at bay from the very beginning. These fish will eat the algae that grow on the sides of the aquarium and on the leaves. Snails will also help to keep the sides of your glass aquarium clean. Algaecides are the chemical way to get rid of algae, but they work on a limited type of algae only. Using natural methods of control are a much better option.

Aquarium Plant Nutrition

The elements of aquarium plant nutrition:

- Aquarium plants require carbon dioxide. They will for instance get carbon dioxide from what fish and other animals excrete during breathing.
- Aquarium plants require oxygen, since their cells burn sugars just like animal cells. Oxygen will be dissolved in the water. Oxygen is also a bi-product of photosynthesis, which is carried out by the plants themselves.
- Aquarium plants require so called macro nutrients. Of these, nitrogen, phosphorus and potassium are the most important ones. Plants must however also get ample amounts of hydrogen, calcium, magnesium, sulfur and iron.
- Aquarium plants need certain micro nutrients, including boron, copper, chlorine, manganese, molybdenum, zinc, and possibly sodium. Most plant species will receive adequate amounts of micro nutrients from the water, from the substrate and from the food you feed your fish.

Sources of Aquarium Plant Nutrition

Tap or Well Water

Some aquarists only use distilled water, or let the water go through extensive deionization and/or reverse osmosis before they use it for their aquariums. A problem with this approach is that you risk removing plenty of beneficial nutrients from the water. For a beginner hobbyist, using normal tap or well water is therefore a better idea. Those who use heavily treated water are normally advanced aquarists that know how to add the necessary nutrients afterwards. If you are not, do not let anyone lure you into buying expensive "special water". Ask a reputable fish store to test your tap or well water and see if it is fit for aquarium use and the species you wish to keep.

Quarium substrates are normally filled with ample amount of plant nutrients in forms that can be readily absorbed by your plants. Different plants have different preferences, and this can be a good idea to take into account before you set up an aquarium. Aquarium gravel can be enhanced in several different ways, e.g. by mixing it with nutritious clay or by using artificial fertilizers for aquarium use.

Every time you add fish food to your aquarium, you add nutrients. (This is one of the main reasons why an aquarium can never be a closed and perfectly balanced eco-system.) Some nutrients will dissolve in the water or sink to the bottom and be directly consumed by the plants. Other nutrients will be eaten by fish first, and then expelled in the form of fish feces than can be used by the plants. fertilization. There are many different types of aquarium fertilizers available today, including liquid fertilizers, granular fertilizers and pellets. Liquid fertilizers are ideal if you have a lot of floating plants and plants anchored to aquarium decoration. Granular fertilizers and pellets will work during a longer period of time and is a good choice if you have a lot of plants planted in the substrate.

Always get aquarium fertilizers, because terrestrial fertilizers can poison the entire aquarium. Terrestrial fertilizers do not match the needs of aquatic plants and the aquatic ecosystem. It does not matter if the terrestrial fertilizer is artificial or natural (uera, bloodmeal etc), it will bring on mayhem either way.

Before you start using artificial fertilizers, keep in mind that fertilization, lighting and carbon dioxide must be balanced if you want to achieve optimal plant growth. Boosting one single factor will not produce any desirable results, and may even cause problems for the other inhabitants of the aquarium.

Water circulation and water changes are important for plants, since it provides them with new nutrients. In the wild, currents, rains, flooding, etcetera continuously provide water circulation and water changes in most habitats. Plants from such habitats will therefore appreciate regular water changes and some type of current/water movement in the aquarium.

Temperature, pH-value and water hardiness are three factors known to affect the amount of available nutrition and how easy it will be for the plants to absorb and make use of that nutrition. You should therefore avoid mixing plant species that want very different temperatures, pH-values and water hardiness levels. Check temperature, pH-value and water hardiness regularly and make sure that the figures stay within the recommended range.

5

Blue Crab

Scientific Classification

Kingdom	:	Animalia
Phylum	:	Arthropoda
Subphylum	:	Crustacea
Class	:	Malacostraca
Order	:	Decapoda
Suborder	:	Pleocyemata
Infraorder	:	Brachyura
Family	:	Portunidae
Genus	:	*Callinectes*
Species	:	*C. sapidus*

Binomial Name

The *blue crab* (*Callinectes sapidus,* from the Greek *calli*= "beautiful", *nectes*= "swimmer", and Latin *sapidus*= "savory") is a crustacean found in the waters of the western Atlantic Ocean and Gulf of Mexico, which is the Maryland State Crustacean and the subject of an extensive fishery. They can deliver an extremely painful pinch and are noted for being particularly aggressive (even out of the water, they will lunge towards movement they consider a threat) and difficult to handle safely.

DISTRIBUTION AND ECOLOGY

The blue crab is native to the western edge of the Atlantic Ocean from Nova Scotia to Argentina.[2] It has been introduced (via ballast water) to Japanese and European waters and has been observed from the Baltic Sea, North Sea, Mediterranean Sea and Black Sea.

The natural predators of the blue crab include eels, drum, spot, trout, some sharks, and cownose sting rays. The blue crab is an omniore, eating both plants and animals. Blue crabs typically consume thin-shelled bivalves, annelids, fish, plants and nearly any other item they can find, including carrion.

Commercial Importance

The Chesapeake Bay, located in Maryland and Virginia, is famous for its blue crabs, and they are one of the most important economic items harvested from it. In 1993, the combined harvest of the blue crabs was valued at around 100 million U.S. dollars. Over the years the harvests of the blue crab dropped in 2000, the combined harvest was around 45 million dollars. Late in the twentieth century, the Maryland Department of Natural Resources created stricter guidelines for harvesting blue crabs to help increase populations These include raising the legal size from 5 to 5¼ inches (from 12.7 to 13.3 cm) and limiting the days and times they may be caught.

While blue crabs remain a popular food in the Chesapeake Bay area, the Bay is not capable of meeting local demand. Most whole blue crabs sold in restaurants in Maryland are shipped into the region from North Carolina, Louisiana, Florida and Texas and many crabcakes are made of crabmeat imported from overseas. At least one well-known "traditional Maryland" seafood restaurant actually imports a Southeast Asian crab, an industry there that employs about 15,000 people.

Harvesting Techniques

Blue crabs are commercially harvested by using a trap known as a "crab pot" (similar to a Lobster pot). The crab pot is made out of wire mesh (older designs of wood and wire also exist, as well as all metal varieties) and is cubical in shape. The crab pot usually contains two "entrances" for the crabs that prohibit exit. These are in the form of a tapered aperture that allows the crab to squeeze through in one direction only. A crab pot is baited with any of several types of meat, including bunker, bluefish, chicken or eel. The bait is placed in a holding compartment, a separate meshed enclosure in the center of the pot which is accessible through a door on the bottom of the crab pot. This design attracts the crabs through the entrances while preventing them from completely removing the bait. The pots are distributed throughout the crabber's harvesting area in long straight lines and are checked approximately once a day for captures or depleted bait. Crabs that are caught are removed, and the pot is re-baited for the next day.

Crabbers sort the crabs into males ("jimmies") and females ("sooks" or "she-crabs"), and further sort the females into those gravid (with eggs) or not. Catch limits for females are more restrictive than for males, and when sold, the buyer will want to know whether he is buying males or females. Those crabs with signs of getting ready to molt or shed are called "busters" and are also separated from the rest, and placed in shedding tanks. These tanks are usually raised and made of concrete blocks, about 3 feet by 5 feet in size. The water is constantly circulated bay or river water, and the crabs are separated into tanks according to the molting stage, determined by a pinkish spot on the swimming fins which gradually turns red, before visible signs of the shell separation are visible. This continual resorting helps prevent the harder shelled crabs from eating the ones that are beginning to actually shed. Once the shed happens, the pressure of the needing-to-be-larger crab helps the shell to crack, and the crab then backs out of the shell. At this point it is extremely vulnerable because the new shell is a gelatinous papery substance which does not protect the crab. Right after shedding, you can observe the crab becoming noticibly larger because the new shell also expands until it hardens, which takes about 48 hours. Crabbers are constantly tending the tank, and after the expansion, the crabs are removed and iced or flash frozen for transportation to market as soft shell crabs. In well tended shedding tanks there is about a 10% mortality rate. If the shedding process is not managed, the mortality can be as high as 50 per cent.

For the recreational crabber, there exist a variety of crab traps. (Recreational crabbers rarely use commercial pots.) The design of a trap can vary widely, but the common varieties are made out of wire mesh. The crab trap is usually cubical or pyramidal in shape although cylindrical designs are also used. The crab trap contains some form of "entrance" for the crabs, such as hinged panels, that are typically closed as the trap is raised from the water. Like the commercial pots, the crab trap is baited with any of several types of meat, chicken usually being the easiest to obtain. The bait is placed in a holding spot in the middle of the trap usually in some form of clip allowing the crab direct access. This design has the potential to more easily allow the crab to escape with the bait but the trap is usually checked frequently enough (every 15 to 30 minutes) to prevent this from happening. Some recreational crabbers add the catch from the traps to a "keeper pot" that holds the live crabs until a substantial harvest is accumulated. When the keeper pot is appreciably full, the contents are prepared for a "crab feast" or for sale.

Crabs can also be caught with a trotline. While this method generally allows one to catch more crabs than other recreational methods, it requires more effort and equipment. This method is used by advanced recreational crabbers and some smaller commercial operations. Other recreational methods involve line crabbing (using a single baited line similar to fishing) or simply wading through the water with a dip net. Crabs can also be taken from a slow-moving motorboat. During the day, crabbers will operate the boat in shallow, grassy waters (flats) and use a long-handled net to scoop them from the bottom, where they can be easily seen moving about. At night, the crabs swim in deeper water. By scanning the water ahead of the boat using a spotlight, the crabs are easily seen and caught.

Preparation

Blue crabs are most often eaten in the hard shell. Steaming them in large pots with water, vinegar and seasoning Old Bay Seasoning is a popular variety in Maryland) is the norm on the East coast. The crabs are placed on a raised tray (with holes for the steam), in large cooking pots similar to pot used for cooking pasta. There is water under the tray. As the crabs are layered into the pot large amounts of the seasoning (usually Old Bay) are sprinkled between the layers. The lid is then placed on the pot and kept at boiling until the crabs turn red-just as lobsters and shrimp also turn red.

However, places like New Orleans tend to boil them in water and heavy cajun seasoning which is similar to boiling crawfish. Stores carry this as "Crab Boil" or "Shrimp Boil" spice, which is added to the water, and the crabs are immersed in the water. Again, they are done when they turn red.

The cooked crabs are cracked by hand, and the meat pulled out and eaten directly. Crab shells are wickedly sharp, so the eater of crabs is going to work for the eating pleasure. Because the interior of the crab is also a series of compartments separated by a somewhat pliable but still sharp shell, getting the meat out is also a lot of work for small amount of edible crab. Crabs are often referred as having a tab, like beer cans have for opening. The male tab is sometimes referred to as the Washington Monument because of the long straight tab, while the tabs on females are referred to as the Jefferson Monument in shape. This tab is pried up and pulled off, which gives you a place to pry the upper and lower shells apart. On the bottom of the crab, you then remove the gills or "devil". There is also the crab's equivalent of a liver and pancreas, which is considered a high delicacy by native crab eaters, but usually removed by those who came to crabs later in life. This is called 'tomalley' or, in Maryland and Virginia, referred to as 'mustar' or 'mustard', probably referring to the color, similar to Dijon mustard.

The picked meat, especially the large chunks from the backfin area, can also be used to make crab cakes, crab soup, or other dishes. Picked crab meat is also sold commercially, and the canning operations have huge crab picking 'houses' usually manned by local women armed with sharp knives and who manage to completely remove the meat, sorted into lump, claw, backfin, and the other smaller bits, in less time than a the usual crab eater takes just to get into one crab, remove the gills, and pry out the lumps. Local Maryland and Virginia crab eaters know not to eat crab cakes-even if labeled "Maryland" anywhere other than in Maryland and Virginia. Larger pieces of meat are preferred by customers, but since they fall apart easily, a cook has to carefully fold in crab meat, rather than stir it. A true crab cake has only a small amount of breading, if any, just enough egg to hold it together, and very little in spice, although over the years, more and more Old Bay spice is being added, which wasn't usually used in crab cakes prior to around 1980s. Traditionally crab cakes were fried, but many people today prefer broiled.

Crabs caught just after molting (before the new shell has had time to harden) are prepared as soft shell crabs. Soft shell crabs are prepared by first cutting out the gills, face, and guts. The crab is then battered in flour, egg, and seasoning, then fried in oil until crispy. The result can be served as an entrée, or in a sandwich. When served between bread slices or crackers, the legs stick out on either side, and the entire crab is consumed, legs and all. Blue crabs average 15% edible meat, and that meat is high in vitamin B_{12}. Just three ounces of crab meat contain a full day's allowance of the vitamin.

The blue crab is one of the most common marine invertebrates in the western Atlantic. The common range of the blue crab is from New England to Florida. Periodic appearances of the blue crab have also been noted in parts of Europe, most likely due to transportation of the species in ships ballast. The blue crab may be found in salt, fresh and brackish waters, but is most prevalent in the latter. The blue crab may grow up to eight inches lengthwise across the shell. Coloring of the crab is blue, blue-green or brown with cream colored markings on top. The bottom of the crab is white with red markings. Once cooked, the crab takes on a scarlet hue.

To some people blue crabs are as much a part of a summer vacation as sun bathing. The blue crab is one of the most common estuarine invertebrates from the Mid-Atlantic to the Gulf of Mexico and supports a tremenduous commercial fishery and a large recreational fishery as well. Commercially crabs are caught either in pots or with trot lines in the warm months when they are active or with dredges during the winter. Crab pots are generally made of wire and, baited with pieces of fresh fish, set in likely spots. The floats that crab fishermen use to locate their pots can be seen dotting our bays in the warmer months of the year. Trotlines are long lines that have regularly spaced baited dropper lines hung from them at intervals. The fisherman runs along the line with his boat, gently lifting the line and netting the crabs that are hanging onto the bait.

Blue crab is prepared either in the hardshell or softshell forms. Hardshell crabs are commonly boiled whole, and served still within their shells. The hard shell is cracked be hand or with the aid of nut crackers. Once the shell has been broken into, nearly the entirety of the crab meat may be consumed.. The meat within the body of the crab is thick and whitish in color, while pieces from the legs are smaller and flakier. Meat from the two large claws is solid and more abundant than meat found in the smaller legs. Softshell crabs are prepared in a different manner, this preparation begun right after the crabs are caught. Softshell crabs are those that have just newly molted. Crabbers will inspect their freshly caught crabs to determine which are about to molt. Those that are about ready are separated from the rest of the crabs and held in shallow tanks supplied with running water until they molt. These crabs are more valuable on the market than hardshell crabs, and after being cooked the entire crab, shell and all, may be consumed.

In the Mid-Atlantic, blue crabs spawn from May until October. The female crab carries millions of eggs in order to compensate for larval high mortality rates. After hatching, the crabs mature quickly, reaching full size within twelve to eighteen months.

Crab "shedding" is a rapidly developing industry that lies somewhere between commercial harvesting and aquaculture. By inspecting the freshly harvested crabs, a fisherman can determine which are within a few days of molting. These pre-molt crabs are segregated and held in shallow tanks supplied with running water until they shed their old shells. The newly molted crabs are called soft-shells and are worth significantly more than their hard-shelled siblings.

6

Shrimp Farm

Introduction

A *shrimp farm* is an aquaculture business for the cultivation of marine shrimp or prawnsa for human consumption. Commercial shrimp farming began in the 1970s, and production grew steeply, particularly to match the market demands of the U.S., Japan and Western Europe. The total global production of farmed shrimp reached more than 1.6 million tonnes in 2003, representing a value of nearly 9,000 million U.S. dollars. About 75% of farmed shrimp is produced in Asia, in particular in China and Thailand. The other 25% is produced mainly in Latin America, where Brazil is the largest producer. The largest exporting nation is Thailand.

Shrimp farming has changed from traditional, small-scale businesses in Southeast Asia into a global industry. Technological advances have led to growing shrimp at ever higher densities, and broodstock is shipped worldwide. Virtually all farmed shrimp are penaeids (i.e., shrimp of the family *Penaeidae*), and just two species of shrimp—the *Penaeus vannamei* (Pacific white shrimp) and the *Penaeus monodon* (giant tiger prawn)—account for roughly 80% of all farmed shrimp. These industrial monocultures are very susceptible to diseases, which have caused several regional wipe-outs of farm shrimp populations. Increasing ecological problems, repeated disease outbreaks, and pressure and criticism from both NGOs and consumer countries led to changes in the industry in the late 1990s and generally stronger regulation by governments. In 1999, a program aimed at developing and promoting more sustainable farming practices was initiated, including governmental bodies, industry representatives, and environmental organizations.

History and Geography

Shrimp have been farmed for centuries in Asia, using traditional low-density methods. Indonesian brackish water ponds called *tambaks* can be traced back as far as the 15th century. Shrimp were farmed on a small scale in ponds, in monocultures or together with other species such as milkfish, or in rotation with rice, using the rice paddies for shrimp cultures during the dry season, when no rice could be grown Such traditional cultures often were small operations in coastal areas or on river banks. Mangrove areas were favoured because of their naturally abundant supply of shrimp Wild juvenile shrimp were trapped in ponds and reared on naturally occurring organisms in the water until they had the desired size and then were harvested.

The origins of industrial shrimp farming can be traced back to the 1930s, when Kuruma shrimp (*Penaeus japonicus*) was spawned and cultivated for the first time in Japan. By the 1960s, a small shrimp farming industry had appeared in Japan ommercial shrimp farming began in the late 1960s and early 1970s. Technological advances led to ever more intensive forms of shrimp farming, and the growing market demand led to a proliferation of shrimp farms throughout the world, concentrated in tropical and sub-tropical regions. The growing consumer demand coincided in the early 1980s with faltering wild shrimp catches, creating a veritable boom in shrimp aquaculture. Taiwan was amongst the early adopters and a major producer in the 1980s; its production collapsed beginning in 1988 due to poor management practices and disease. In Thailand, large-scale intensive shrimp farming expanded rapidly from 1985 In South America, shrimp farming was pioneered by Ecuador, where it expanded dramatically from 1978. Brazil had been active in shrimp farming since 1974, but the trade really boomed there only in the 1990s, making the country a major producer within a few years. Today, there are marine shrimp farms in over fifty countries.

Farming Methods

When shrimp farming emerged in the 1970s as an economically viable alternative to satisfy growing market demands that had surpassed the capacity of the wild shrimp fishery, the subsistence farming methods of old were rapidly replaced by the more intensive practices of an export-oriented business. Industrial shrimp farming at first followed these traditional methods with so-called extensive shrimp farms, but compensated for the low yield per area with increased pond sizes: instead of ponds of just a few hectares, ponds of sizes up to 100 ha (one km^2) were used in some places. The initially largely unregulated business boomed, and in many regions whole coastlines were transformed and huge areas of mangroves cleared. Further technological advances made more intensive farming practices possible that could achieve higher yields per area while using less land. Semi-intensive and intensive farms appeared, where the shrimp were reared on artificial feeds and ponds were actively managed. Although there are still many extensive farms, new farms typically are of the (semi-)intensive kind.

Until the mid-1980s, most shrimp farms were stocked with young wild shrimp, called *postlarvae*, typically caught by local fishermen. Postlarvae fishing became an important economic sector in many countries. To counteract the beginning depletion of fishing grounds and to ensure a steady supply of young shrimp to farms, the industry started raising shrimp from the egg and maintaining adult shrimp for reproductive purposes in specialized installations called hatcheries.

Life Cycle of Shrimp

Shrimp mature and breed only in a marine habitat. The females lay 50,000 to 1 million eggs, which hatch after some 24 hours into tiny nauplii. These nauplii feed on yolk reserves within their body and then undergo a metamorphosis into zoeae. This second larval stage feeds in the wild on algae and after a few days metamorphoses again into the third stage to become myses. The myses already look akin to tiny shrimp and feed on algae and zooplankton. After another three to four days they metamorphose a final time into postlarvae: young shrimp having all the characteristics of adults. The whole process takes about 12 days from hatching. In the wild, the postlarvae then migrate into estuaries, which are rich in nutrients and low in salinity. There they grow and eventually migrate back into open waters when they mature. Adult shrimp are benthic animals living primarily on the sea bottom.

Technologies

In shrimp farming, this lifecycle occurs under controlled conditions. The reasons to do so include more intensive farming, improved size control resulting in more uniformly sized shrimp, and better predator control, but also the ability to speed up the cycle by controlling the climate (especially in farms in the temperate zones, using greenhouses). There are three different stages:

- *Hatcheries* breed shrimp and produce nauplii or even postlarvae, which they sell to farms. Large shrimp farms maintain their own hatcheries and sell nauplii or postlarvae to smaller farms in the region.
- *Nurseries* are those parts of a shrimp farm where postlarvae are grown and accustomed to the marine conditions in the growout ponds.
- In the *growout* ponds the shrimp are grown from juveniles to marketable size, which takes between three to six months.

Most farms produce one to two harvests a year; in tropical climates, a farm may even produce three. Because of the need for salt water, shrimp farms are located on or near a coast. Inland shrimp farms have also been tried in some regions, but the need to ship salt water and competition for land with agricultural users led to problems. Thailand banned inland shrimp farms in 1999.

Hatcheries

Small-scale hatcheries are very common throughout Southeast Asia. Often run as family businesses and using a low-technology approach, they use small tanks (less than ten tons) and often low animal densities. They are susceptible to disease, but due to their small size, they can typically restart production quickly after disinfection. The survival rate is anywhere between zero and 90%, depending on a wide range of factors, including disease, the weather, and the experience of the operator.

Greenwater hatcheries are medium-sized hatcheries using large tanks with low animal densities. To feed the shrimp larvae, an algal bloom is induced in the tanks. The survival rate is about 40%.

Galveston hatcheries (named after Galveston, Texas, where they were developed) are large-scale, industrial hatcheries using a closed and tightly controlled environment. They breed the shrimp at high densities in large (15 to 30 ton) tanks. Survival rates vary between zero and 80%, but typically achieve 50%.

In hatcheries, the developing shrimp are fed on a diet of algae and later also brine shrimp nauplii, sometimes (especially in industrial hatcheries) augmented by artificial diets. The diet of later stages also includes fresh or freeze-dried animal protein, for example krill. Nutrition and medication (such as antibiotics) fed to the brine shrimp nauplii are passed on to the shrimp that eat them.

Many farms have nurseries where the postlarval shrimp are grown into juveniles for another three weeks in separate ponds, tanks, or so-called raceways. A raceway is a rectangular, long, shallow tank through which water flows continuously.

In a typical nursery, there are 150 to 200 animals per square metre. They are fed on a high-protein diet for at most about three weeks before they are moved to the growout ponds. At that time, they weigh between one and two grams. The water salinity is adjusted gradually to that of the growout ponds.

Farmers refer to postlarvae as "PLs", with the number of days suffixed (i.e., PL-1, PL-2, etc.). They are ready to be transferred to the growout ponds after their gills have branched, which occurs around PL-13 to PL-17 (about 25 days after hatching). Nursing is not absolutely necessary, but is favored by many farms because it makes for better food utilization, improves the size uniformity, helps utilize the infrastructure better, and can be done in a controlled environment to increase the harvest. The main disadvantage of nurseries is that some of the postlarval shrimp die upon the transfer to the growout pond.

Some farms do not use a nursery but stock the postlarvae directly in the growout ponds after having acclimated them to the appropriate temperature and salinity levels in an acclimation tank. Over the course of a few days, the water in these tanks is changed gradually to match that of the growout ponds. The animal density should not exceed 500/litre for young postlarvae and 50/litre for larger ones, such as PL-15.

Shrimp pond with paddlewheel aerators in Indonesia. The pond is in an early stage of cultivation; plankton has been seeded and grown (whence the greenish color of the water); shrimp fry is to be released next.

In the growout phase, the shrimp are grown to maturity. The postlarvae are transferred to ponds where they are fed until they reach marketable size, which takes about another three to six months. Harvesting the shrimp is done by fishing them from the ponds using nets or by draining the ponds. Pond sizes and the level of technical infrastructure vary.

Extensive shrimp farms using traditional low-density methods are invariably located on a coast and often in mangrove areas. The ponds range from just a few to more than 100 hectares; shrimp are stocked at low densities (2–3 animals per square metre, or 25,000/ha). The tides provide for some water exchange, and the shrimp feed on naturally occurring organisms. In some areas, farmers even grow wild shrimp by just opening the gates and impounding wild larvae. Prevalent in poorer or less developed countries where land prices are low, extensive farms produce annual yields from 50 to 500 kg/ha of shrimp (head-on weight). They have low production costs (US$1–3/kg live shrimp), are not very labor intensive, and do not require advanced technical skills.

Semi-intensive farms do not rely on tides for water exchange but use pumps and a planned pond layout. They can therefore be built above the high tide line. Pond sizes range from 2 to 30 ha; the stocking densities range from 10 to 30/m^2 (100,000–300,000/ha). At such densities, artificial feeding using industrially prepared shrimp feeds and fertilizing the pond to stimulate the growth of naturally occurring organisms become a necessity. Annual yields range from 500 to 5,000 kg/ha, while production costs are in the range of US$2–6/kg live shrimp. With densities above 15 animals per square metre, aeration is often required to prevent oxygen depletion. Productivity varies depending upon water temperature, thus it is common to have larger sized shrimp in some seasons than in others.

The intake of a two-horsepower "Turbo aerator", which paddles one metre below the water surface. To avoid stirring up pond sediments, the water depth should be at least 1.5 m.

Intensive farms use even smaller ponds (0.1–1.5 ha) and even higher stocking densities. The ponds are actively managed: they are aerated, there is a high water exchange to remove waste products and maintain water quality, and the shrimp are fed on specially designed diets, typically in the form of formulated pellets. Such farms produce annual yields between 5,000 and 20,000 kg/ha; a few super-intensive farms can produce as much as 100,000 kg/ha. They require an advanced technical infrastructure and highly trained professionals for constant monitoring of water quality and other pond conditions; their production costs are in the range of US$4–8/kg live shrimp.

Estimates on the production characteristics of shrimp farms vary. Most studies agree that about 55–60% of all shrimp farms worldwide are extensive farms, another 25–30% are semi-intensive, the rest being intensive farms. Regional variation is high, though, and reports wide discrepancies in the percentages claimed for individual countries by different studies.

Feeding the Shrimps

While extensive farms mainly rely on the natural productivity of the ponds, more intensively managed farms rely on artificial shrimp feeds, either exclusively or as a supplement to the organisms that naturally occur in a pond. A food chain is established in the ponds, based on the growth of phytoplankton. Fertilizers and mineral conditioners are used to boost the growth of the phytoplankton to accelerate the growth of the shrimps. Waste from the artificial food pellets and excrements of the shrimps can lead to the eutrophication of the ponds.

Artificial feeds come in the form of specially formulated, granulated pellets that disintegrate quickly. Up to 70% of such pellets are wasted, as they decay before the shrimps have eaten them The shrimps are fed two to five times daily; the feeding can be done manually either from ashore or from boats, or using mechanized feeders distributed all over a pond. The feed conversion rate (FCR), i.e. the amount of food needed to produce a unit (e.g. one kilogram) of shrimp, is claimed by the industry to be around 1.2–2 in modern farms, but this is an optimum value that is not always attained in practice. For a farm to be profitable, a feed conversion rate below 2.5 is necessary; in older farms or under suboptimal pond conditions, the ratio may easily rise to 4:1. Lower FCRs result in a higher profit for the farm.

Farmed Species

Although there are many species of shrimp and prawn, only a few of the larger ones are actually cultivated, all of which belong to the family of penaeids (family Penaeidae), and within it to the genus *Penaeus*c. Many species are unsuitable for farming: they are too small to be profitable, or simply stop growing when crowded together, or are too susceptible to diseases. The two species dominating the market are:

- Pacific white shrimp (*Litopenaeus vannamei,* also called "whiteleg shrimp") is the main species cultivated in western countries. Native to the Pacific coast from Mexico to Peru, it grows to a size of 23 cm. *P. vannamei* accounts for 95% of the production in Latin America. It is easy to breed in captivity, but succumbs to the Taura disease.
- Giant tiger prawn (*P. monodon,* also known as "black tiger shrimp") occurs in the wild in the Indian Ocean and in the Pacific Ocean from Japan to Australia. The largest of all

the cultivated shrimp, it can grow to a length of 36 cm and is farmed in Asia. Because of its susceptibility to whitespot disease and the difficulty of breeding it in captivity, it is gradually being replaced by *L. vannamei* since 2001.

Together, these two species account for about 80% of the whole farmed shrimp production. Other species being bred are:

- Western blue shrimp (*P. stylirostris*) was a popular choice for shrimp farming in the western hemisphere, until the IHHN virus wiped out nearly the whole population in the late 1980s. A few stocks survived and became resistant against this virus. When it was discovered that some of these were also resistant against the Taura virus, some farms again bred *P. stylirostris* from 1997 on.
- Chinese white shrimp (*P. chinensis*, also known as the *fleshy prawn*) occurs along the coast of China and the western coast of Korea and is being farmed in China. It grows to a maximum length of only 18 cm, but tolerates colder water (min. 16°C). Once a major factor on the world market, it is today used almost exclusively for the Chinese domestic market after a disease wiped out nearly all the stocks in 1993.
- Kuruma shrimp (*P. japonicus*) is farmed primarily in Japan and Taiwan, but also in Australia; the only market is in Japan, where live Kuruma shrimp reach prices of the order of US$100 per pound ($220/kg).
- Indian white shrimp (*P. indicus*) is a native of the coasts of the Indian Ocean and is widely bred in India, Iran and the Middle East and along the African shores.
- Banana shrimp (*P. merguiensis*) is another cultured species from the coastal waters of the Indian Ocean, from Oman to Indonesia and Australia. It can be grown at high densities.

Several other species of *Penaeus* play only a very minor role in shrimp farming. Some other kinds of shrimp also can be farmed, e.g. the "Akiami paste shrimp" or *Metapenaeus spp.* Their total production from aquaculture is of the order of only about 25,000 tonnes per year, small in comparison to that of the penaeids.

Diseases

There are a variety of lethal viral diseases that affect shrimp. In the densely populated, monocultural farms such virus infections spread rapidly and may wipe out whole shrimp populations. A major transfer vector of many of these viruses is the water itself; and thus any virus outbreak also carries the danger of decimating shrimp living in the wild.

Yellowhead disease, called *Hua leung* in Thai, affects *P. monodon* throughout Southeast Asia. had been reported first in Thailand in 1990. The disease is highly contagious and leads to mass mortality within 2 to 4 days. The cephalothorax of an infected shrimp turns yellow after a period of unusually high feeding activity ending abruptly, and the then moribund shrimp congregate near the surface of their pond before dying.

Whitespot syndrome is a disease caused by a family of related viruses. First reported in 1993 from Japanese *P. japonicus* cultures it spread throughout Asia and then to the Americas. It has a wide host range and is highly lethal, leading to mortality rates of 100% within days. Symptoms include white spots on the carapace and a red hepatopancreas. Infected shrimp become lethargic before they die.

Taura syndrome was first reported from shrimp farms on the Taura river in Ecuador in 1992. The host of the virus causing the disease is *P. vannamei,* one of the two most commonly farmed shrimp. The disease spread rapidly, mainly through the shipping of infected animals and broodstock. Originally confined to farms in the Americas, it has also been propagated to Asian shrimp farms with the introduction of *P. vannamei* there. Birds are thought to be a route of infection between farms within one region.

Infectious Hypodermal and Hematopoietic Necrosis (IHHN) is a disease that causes mass mortality among *P. stylirostris* (as high as 90%) and severe deformations in *P. vannamei.* It occurs in Pacific farmed and wild shrimp, but not in wild shrimp on the Atlantic coast of the Americas.

There are also a number of bacterial infections that are lethal to shrimp. The most common is vibriosis, caused by the bacterium *Vibrio* sp. The shrimp become weak and disoriented and may have dark wounds on the cuticle. The mortality rate can exceed 70%. Another bacterial disease is Necrotising hepatopancreatitis (NHP); symptoms include a soft exoskeleton and fouling. Most such bacterial infections are strongly correlated to stressful conditions such as overcrowded ponds, high temperatures, and poor water quality: factors that positively influence the growth of bacteria. Treatment is done using antibiotics Importing countries have repeatedly placed import bans on shrimp containing various antibiotics. One such antibiotic is chloramphenicol, which has been banned in the European Union since 1994, but continues to pose problems.

With their high mortality rates, diseases represent a very real danger to shrimp farmers, who may lose their income for the whole year if their ponds are infected. Since most diseases cannot yet be treated effectively, the industry's efforts are focused on preventing diseases to break out in the first place. Active water quality management helps avoid poor pond conditions favourable to the spread of diseases, and instead of using larvae from wild catches, specific pathogen free broodstocks raised in captivity in isolated environments and certified not to carry diseases are used increasingly. To avoid introducing diseases into such disease-free populations on a farm, there is also a trend to create more controlled environments in the ponds of (semi-) intensive farms, such as by lining them with plastic to avoid soil contact, and by minimizing water exchange in the ponds.

Economy

The total global production of farmed shrimp reached more than 1.6 million tonnes in 2003, representing a farm-gate value of nearly 9 billion U.S. dollars This accounts for 25% of the total shrimp production that year (farming and wild catches combined) The largest market for shrimp is the United States, importing more than 500,000 tonnes of shrimp in 2003. About 250,000 tonnes went to Japan, while the four major European shrimp importing countries (France, Spain, the UK, and Italy) imported together about another 500,000 tonnes.

The import prices for shrimp fluctuate wildly. In 2003 the import priçe per kilogram shrimp in the United States was US$ 8.80, slightly higher than in Japan at US$8. The average import price in the EU was only about US$5/kg; this much lower value is explained by the fact that the EU imports more coldwater shrimp (from catches) that are much smaller than the farmed warm water species and thus attain lower prices. In addition, Mediterranean Europe prefers head-on shrimp which weigh approximately 30% more but have a lower unit price.

About 75% of the world production of farmed shrimp comes from Asian countries; the two leading nations being China and Thailand, closely followed by Vietnam, Indonesia, and India. The other 25% are produced in the western hemisphere, where the South-American countries (Brazil, Ecuador, Mexico) dominate. In terms of export, Thailand is by far the leading nation with a market share of more than 30%, followed by China, Indonesia, and India, accounting each for about 10%. Other major export nations are Vietnam, Bangladesh, and Ecuador Thailand exports nearly all of its production, while China uses most of its shrimp in the domestic market. The only other major export nation that has a strong domestic market for farmed shrimp is Mexico.

Disease problems have repeatedly impacted the shrimp production negatively. Besides the near-wipeout of *P. chinensis* in 1993, there were outbreaks of viral diseases that led to marked declines in the per-country production in 1996-97 in Thailand and repeatedly in Ecuador. In Ecuador alone, production suffered heavily in 1989 (IHHN), 1993 (Taura), and 1999 (whitespot). Another reason for sometimes wild changes in shrimp farm output are the import regulations of the destination countries, which do not allow shrimp contaminated by chemicals or antibiotics to be imported.

In the 1980s and through much of the 1990s, shrimp farming promised high profits. The investments required for extensive farms were low, especially in regions with low land prices and wages. For many tropical countries, especially those with poorer economies, shrimp farming was an attractive business, offering jobs and incomes for poor coastal populations and has, due to the high market prices of shrimp, provided many developing countries with non-negligible foreign currency earnings. Many shrimp farms were funded initially by the World Bank or substantially subsidized by local governments.

In the late 1990s, the economic situation changed. Governments and farmers alike were under increasing pressure from NGOs and the consumer countries, who criticized the practices of the trade. International trade conflicts erupted, such as import bans by consumer countries on shrimp containing antibiotics, the United States' shrimp import ban against Thailand in 2004 as a measure against Thai shrimp *fishers* not using Turtle Excluder Devices in their nets or the "anti-dumping" case initiated by U.S. shrimp fishers in 2002 against shrimp farmers worldwide, which resulted two years later in the U.S. imposing anti-dumping tariffs of the order of about 10% against many producer countries (except China, which received a 112% duty). Diseases caused significant economic losses. In Ecuador, where shrimp farming was a major export sector (the other two are Bananas and Oil), the whitespot outbreak of 1999 caused an estimated 130,000 workers to lose their jobs. urthermore, shrimp prices dropped sharply in 2000. All of these factors contributed to the slowly growing acceptance by farmers that improved farming practices were needed, and resulted in tighter government regulation of the business, both of which internalized some of the external costs that were ignored during the boom years.

Socio-economic Aspects

Shrimp farming offers significant employment opportunities, which may help alleviate the poverty of the local coastal populations in many areas, if it is properly managed. The published literature on that topic shows large discrepancies, and much of the available data is of anecdotal nature Estimates of the labor-intensiveness of shrimp farms range from about three times less to three times more than when the same area was used for rice paddies, with much regional variation and depending on the type of farms surveyed. In general, intensive shrimp farming requires more labour per unit area than extensive farming. Extensive farms cover much more land area and are often but not always located in areas where no agricultural land uses are possible. Supporting industries such as feed production or storage, handling, and trade companies should also not be neglected, even if not all of them are exclusive to shrimp farming.

Typically, workers on a shrimp farm can get better wages than with other employments. A global estimate from one study is that a shrimp farm worker can earn 1.5 – 3 times as much as in other jobs; study from India arrived at a salary increase of about 1.6, and a report from Mexico states that the lowest paid job at shrimp farms was paid in 1996 at 1.22 times the average worker salary in the country.

NGOs have frequently criticized that most of the profits went to large conglomerates instead of to the local population. While this may be true in certain regions such as Ecuador, where most shrimp farms are owned by large companies, it does not apply in all cases. For instance in Thailand, most farms are owned by small local entrepreneurs, although there is a trend to vertically integrate the industries related to shrimp farming from feed producers to food processors and trade companies. A 1994 study reported that a farmer in Thailand could increase his income by a factor of ten by switching from growing rice to farming shrimp. An Indian study from 2003 arrives at similar figures for shrimp farming in the East Godavari district in Andhra Pradesh, India.

Whether the local population benefits from shrimp farming is also dependent on the availability of sufficiently trained people. Extensive farms tend to offer mainly seasonal jobs during harvest that do not require much training. In Ecuador, many of these positions are known to have been filled by migrant workers. More intensive farms have a need for year-round labour in more sophisticated jobs.

Marketing

For commercialization, shrimps are graded and marketed in different categories. From complete shrimps (known as "head-on, shell-on" or HOSO) to peeled and deveined (P&D), any presentation is available in stores. The animals are graded by their size uniformity and then also by their count per weight unit, with larger shrimps attaining higher prices.

Ecological Impacts

The shrimp farms appear as rows of rectangles. In the older image, mangrove swamps wander through the estuaries of several rivers as they reach the Pacific coast. At least one major shrimp farm can be seen in this scene in the upper left quadrant, verifying that shrimp farming was already underway at the time. By 1999 much of the region had been converted to blocks of shrimp ponds.

Shrimp farms of all types, from extensive to super-intensive, can cause severe ecological problems wherever they are located. For extensive farms, huge areas of mangroves were cleared, reducing biodiversity. During the 1980s and 1990s, about 35% of the world's mangrove forests have vanished. Shrimp farming was a major cause of this, accounting for over a third of it according to one study; other studies report between 5% and 10% globally, with enormous regional variability. Other causes of mangrove destruction are population pressure, logging, pollution from other industries, or conversion to other uses such as salt pans Mangroves, through their roots, help stabilize a coastline and capture sediments; their removal has led to a marked increase of erosion and less protection against floods. Mangrove estuaries are also especially rich and productive ecosystems and provide the spawning grounds for many species of fish, including many commercially important ones Many countries have protected their mangroves and forbidden the construction of new shrimp farms in tidal or mangrove areas. The enforcement of the respective laws is often problematic, though, and especially in the least developed countries such as Bangladesh, Myanmar, or Vietnam the conversion of mangroves to shrimp farms remains an issue.

Intensive farms, while reducing the direct impact on the mangroves, have other problems. Their nutrient-rich effluents (industrial shrimp feeds disintegrate quickly, as little as 30% are actually eaten by the shrimp with a corresponding economic loss to the farmer, the rest is wasted are typically discharged into the environment, seriously upsetting the ecological balance. These waste waters contain significant amounts of chemical fertilizers, pesticides, and antibiotics that cause pollution of the environment. Furthermore, releasing antibiotics in such ways injects them into the food chain and increases the risks of bacteria becoming resistant against them However, most aquatic bacteria, unlike bacteria associated with terrestrial animals, are not zoonotic. Only a few disease transfers from animals to humans have been reported.

A toxic sludge oozing out of the bottom of a shrimp pond of a farm in Indonesia after the harvest. The liquid pictured here contained sulfuric acid resulting from oxidation of pyrite contained in the soil. Such contamination of a pond leads to stunted growth of the shrimp and increased mortality rates; the growth of the plankton is reduced drastically. Liming can be applied to counteract to some extent the acidification of the water in ponds on acid sulfate soil such as mangrove soils.

Prolonged use of a pond can lead to an incremental build-up of a sludge at the pond's bottom from waste products and excrements. The sludge can be removed mechanically or dried and plowed to allow bio-decomposition, at least in areas without acid problems. Flushing a pond never completely removes this sludge, and eventually, the pond is abandoned, leaving behind a wasteland with the soil made unusable for any other purposes due to the high levels of salinity, acidity, and toxic chemicals. A typical pond in an extensive farm can be used only a few years. An Indian study estimated the time to rehabilitate such lands to about 30 years. Thailand has banned inland shrimp farms since 1999 because they caused too much destruction of agricultural lands due to salination. A Thai study estimated that 60% of the shrimp farming area in Thailand was abandoned in the years 1989 – 1996. Much of these problems stem from using mangrove land that has high natural pyrite content (acid sulfate soil) and poor drainage. The shift to semi-intensive farming requires higher elevations for drain harvesting and low sulfide (pyrite) content to prevent acid formation when the soils shift from anaerobic to aerobic conditions.

The global nature of the shrimp farming business and in particular the shipment of broodstock and hatchery products throughout the world have not only introduced various shrimp species as exotic species, but also distributed the diseases the shrimp may carry worldwide. As a consequence, most broodstock shipment require health certificates and/or to be SPF (specific pathogen free) status. Many organizations lobby actively for consumers to avoid buying farmed shrimp; some also advocate the development of more sustainable farming methods A joint programme of the World Bank, the Network of Aquaculture Centres in Asia-Pacific (NACA), the WWF, and the FAO was established in August 1999 to study and propose improved practices for shrimp farming Some existing attempts at sustainable export-oriented shrimp farming marketing the shrimp as "ecologically produced" are criticized by NGOs as being dishonest and trivial window-dressing.

Yet the industry has been slowly changing since about 1999. It has adopted the "best management practices" developed by e.g. the World Bank *et al.* programme and instituted educational programmes to promote them. ue to the mangrove protection laws enacted in many countries, new farms are usually of the (semi-)intensive kind, which are best constructed outside of mangrove areas anyway. There is a trend to create even more tightly controlled environments in these farms with the hope to achieve better disease prevention Waste water treatment has attracted considerable attention; modern shrimp farms routinely have effluent treatment ponds where sediments are allowed to settle at the bottom and other residuals are filtered. As such improvements are costly, the World Bank *et al.* programme also recommends low-intensity polyculture farming for some areas. Since it has been discovered that mangrove soils are effective in filtering waste waters and tolerate high nitrate levels, the industry has also developed an interest in mangrove reforestation, although its contributions in that area are still minor. The long-term effects of these recommendations and industry trends cannot be evaluated conclusively yet.

Social Changes

Shrimp farming in many cases has far-reaching effects on the local coastal population. Especially in the boom years of the

1980s and 1990s, when the business was largely unregulated in many countries, the very fast expansion of the industry caused significant changes that sometimes were detrimental to the local population. Conflicts can be traced back to two root causes: competition for common resources such as land and water, and changes induced by wealth redistribution.

A significant problem causing much conflict in some regions, for instance in Bangladesh, are the land use rights. With shrimp farming, a new industry expanded into coastal areas and started to make exclusive use of previously public resources. In some areas, the rapid expansion resulted in the local coastal population being denied access to the coast by a continuous strip of shrimp farms with serious impacts on the local fisheries. Such problems were compounded by poor ecological practices that caused a degradation of common resources (such as excessive use of freshwater to control the salinity of the ponds, causing the water table to sink and leading to the salination of freshwater aquifers by an inflow of salt water). With growing experience, countries usually introduced stronger governmental regulations and have taken steps to mitigate such problems, for instance through land zoning legislations. Some late adopters have even managed to avoid some problems through proactive legislation, e.g. Mexico The situation in Mexico is unique owing to the strongly government-regulated market. Even after the liberalisation in the early 1990s, most shrimp farms are still owned and controlled by locals or local co-ops.

Social tensions have occurred due to changes in the wealth distribution within populations. The effects of this are mixed, though, and the problems are not unique to shrimp farming. Changes in the distribution of wealth tend to induce changes in the power structure within a community. In some cases, there is a widening gap between the general population and local élites who have easier access to credits, subsidies, and permits and thus are more likely to become shrimp farmers and benefit more In Bangladesh, on the other hand, local élites were opposing shrimp farming, which was controlled largely by an urban élite. Land concentrations in a few hands has been recognized to carry an increased risk of social and economic problems developing, especially if the landowners are non-local.

In general, it has been found that shrimp farming is accepted best and introduced most easily and with the greatest benefits for the local communities if the farms are owned by local people instead of by restricted remote élites or large companies because local owners have a direct interest in maintaining the environment and good relations with their neighbors, and because it avoids the formation of large-scale land property.

7

The Mode of Fish Farming

Introduction

Fish farming is the principal form of aquaculture, while other methods may fall under mariculture. It involves raising fish commercially in tanks or enclosures, usually for food. A facility that releases juvenile fish into the wild for recreational fishing or to supplement a species' natural numbers is generally referred to as a fish hatchery. Fish species raised by fish farms include salmon, catfish, tilapia, cod, carp, trout and others.

Increasing demands on wild fisheries by commercial fishing has caused widespread overfishing. Fish farming offers an alternative solution to the increasing market demand for fish and fish protein.

Major Categories of Fish Farms

There are two kinds of aquaculture: extensive aquaculture based on local photosynthetical production and intensive aquaculture, in which the fish are fed with external food supply. The management of these two kinds of aquaculture systems are completely different.

Extensive (pond) Aquaculture

Limiting for growth here is the available food supply by natural sources, commonly zooplankton feeding on pelagic algae or benthic animals, such as certain crustaceans and mollusks.

Tilapia species filter feed directly on phytoplankton, which makes higher production possible. The photosynthetical production can be increased by fertilizing the pond water with artificial fertilizer mixtures, such as potash, phosphorus, nitrogen and microelements. Because most fish are carnivorous, they occupy a higher place in the trophic chain and therefore only a tiny fraction of primary photosynthetic production (typically 1%) will be converted into harvestable fish. As a result, without additional feeding the fish harvest will not exceed 200 kilograms of fish per hectare per year, equivalent to 1% of the gross photosynthetic production.

A second point of concern is the risk of algal blooms. When temperatures, nutrient supply and available sunlight are optimal for algal growth, algae multiply their biomass at an exponential rate, eventually leading to an exhaustion of available nutrients and a subsequent die-off. The decaying algal biomass will deplete the oxygen in the pond water because it blocks out the sun and pollute it with organic and inorganic solutes (such as ammonium ions), which can (and frequently do) lead to massive loss of fish.

In order to tap all available food sources in the pond, the aquaculturist will choose fish species which occupy different places in the pond ecosystem, e.g., a filter algae feeder such as tilapia, a benthic feeder such as carp or catfish and a zooplankton feeder (various carps) or submerged weeds feeder such as grass carp.

Intensive (closed-circulation) Aquaculture

In these kinds of systems fish production per unit of surface can be increased at will, as long as sufficient oxygen, fresh water and food are provided. Because of the requirement of sufficient fresh water, a massive water purification system must be integrated in the fish farm. A clever way to achieve this is the combination of hydroponic horticulture and water treatment, see below. The exception to this rule are cages which are placed in a river or sea, which supplements the fish crop with sufficient fresh water. Environmentalists object to this practice.

The cost of inputs per unit of fish weight is higher than in extensive farming, especially because of the high cost of fish food, which must contain a much higher level of protein (up to 60%) than, e.g., cattle food and a balanced amino acid composition as well. This frequently is offset by the lower land costs and the higher productions which can be obtained due to the high level of input control.

Essential here is aeration of the water, as fish need a sufficient oxygen level for growth. This is achieved by bubbling, cascade flow or aqueous oxygen. Catfish, Clarias ssp. can breathe atmospheric air and can tolerate much higher levels of pollutants than, e.g., trout or salmon, which makes aeration and water purification less necessary and makes *Clarias* species especially suited for intensive fish production. In some *Clarias* farms about 10% of the water volume can consist of fish biomass.

Especially when fish densities are high, the risk of infections by parasites like fish lice, fungi (*Saprolegnia* sp.), intestinal worms (such as nematodes or trematodes), bacteria (e.g., Yersinia ssp, Pseudomonas ssp.), and protozoa (such as Dinoflagellates) is much higher than in animal husbandry because of the ease in which pathogens can invade the fish body (e.g. by the gills). The same holds for water pollution or depletion of oxygen in the water, which can ruin a fish crop within minutes. This means, intensive aquaculture requires tight monitoring and a high level of expertise of the fish farmer.

Intensive aquaculture was developed as a source for food fish. Raising ornamental cold water fish (goldfish or koi), although theoretically much more profitable due to the higher income per weight of fish produced, has never been successfully carried out until very recently. The increased incidences of dangerous viral diseases of koi Carp, together with the high value of the fish has led to initiatives in closed system koi breeding and growing in a number of countries. Today there are a few commercially successful intensive koi growing facilities in the U.K., Germany and Israel.

Some producers have adapted their intensive systems in an effort to provide consumers with fish that do not carry dormant forms of viruses and diseases.

Specific Types of Fish Farms

Within intensive and extensive aquaculture methods there are numerous specific types of fish farms, each has benefits and applications unique to its design.

Integrated Recycling Systems

One of the largest problems with freshwater aquaculture is that it can use a million gallons of water per acre (about 1 m^3 of water per m^2) each year. Extended water purification systems allow for the reuse (recycling) of local water.

The largest-scale pure fish farms use a system derived (admittedly much refined) from the New Alchemists in the 1970s. Basically, large plastic fish tanks are placed in a greenhouse. A hydroponic bed is placed near, above or between them. When tilapia are raised in the tanks, they are able to eat algae, which naturally grows in the tanks when the tanks are properly fertilized.

The tank water is slowly circulated to the hydroponic beds where the tilapia waste feeds a commercial plant crops. Carefully cultured microorganisms in the hydroponic bed convert ammonia to nitrates, and the plants are fertilized by the nitrates and phosphates. Other wastes are strained out by the hydroponic media, which doubles as an aerated pebble-bed filter.

This system, properly tuned, produces more edible protein per unit area than any other. A wide variety of plants can grow well in the hydroponic beds. Most growers concentrate on herbs (e.g. parsley and basil), which command premium prices in small quantities all year long. The most common customers are restaurant wholesalers. Since the system lives in a greenhouse, it adapts to almost all temperate climates, and may also adapt to tropical climates.

The main environmental impact is discharge of water that must be salted to maintain the fishes' electrolyte balance. Current growers use a variety of proprietary tricks to keep fish healthy, reducing their expenses for salt and waste water discharge permits. Some veterinary authorities speculate that ultraviolet ozone disinfectant systems (widely used for ornamental fish) may play a prominent part in keeping the Tilapia healthy with recirculated water.

Irrigation Ditch or Pond Systems

These use irrigation ditches or farm ponds to raise fish. The basic requirement is to have a ditch or pond that retains water, possibly with an above-ground irrigation system (many irrigation systems use buried pipes with headers. Using this method, one can store one's water allotment in ponds or ditches, usually lined with bentonite clay. In small systems the fish are often fed commercial fish food, and their waste products can help fertilize the fields. In larger ponds, the pond grows water plants and algae as fish food. Some of the most successful ponds grow introduced strains of plants, as well as introduced strains of fish.

Control of water quality is crucial. Fertilizing, clarifying and pH control of the water can increase yields substantially, as long as eutrophication is prevented and oxygen levels stay high.Yields can be low if the fish grow ill from electrolyte stress.

Cage System

Fish cages are placed in open water resources to contain and protect fish until they can be harvested. They can be constructed of a wide variety of components. Fishes are stocked in cages, artificially fed, and harvested when they reach market size. A few advantages of fish farming with cages are that many types of waters can be used (rivers, lakes, filled quarries, etc.), many types of fishes can be raised, and fish farming can co-exist with sport fishing and other water uses. Cage farming of fishes in open seas are also gaining popularity. Concerns of disease, poaching, poor water quality, etc., lead some to believe that in general, pond systems are easier to manage and simpler to start. Also, past occurrences of cage-failures leading to escapes, have raised concern regarding the culture of non-native fish species in open-water cages. Even though the cage-industry has made numerous technological advances in cage construction in recent years, the concern for escapes remains valid.

Classic Fry Farming

Trout and other sport fish are often raised from eggs to fry or fingerlings and then trucked to streams and released. Normally, the fry are raised in long, shallow concrete tanks, fed with fresh stream water. The fry receive commercial fish food in pellets. While not as efficient as the New Alchemists' method, it is also far simpler, and has been used for many years to stock streams with sport fish. European eel (*Anguilla anguilla*) aquaculturalists procure a limited supply of glass eels, juvenile stages of the European eel which swim north from the Sargasso Sea breeding grounds, for their farms. The European eel is threatened with extinction because of the excessive catch of glass eels by Spanish fishermen and overfishing of adult eels in, e.g., the Dutch IJsselmeer, Netherlands. As per 2005, no one has managed to breed the European eel in captivity.

The issue of feeds in fish farming has been a controversial one. Many cultured fishes (tilapia, carp, catfish, many others) require no meat or fish products in their diets. Top-level carnivores (Most salmon species) depend on fish feed of which a portion is usually derived from wild caught fish (anchovies, menhaden, etc.). Vegetable-derived proteins have successfully replaced fish meal in feeds for carnivorous fishes, but vegetable-derived oils have not successfully been incorporated into the diets of carnivores.

Secondly, farmed fish are kept in concentrations never seen in the wild (e.g. 50,000 fish in a two-acre area. with each fish occupying less room than the average bathtub. This can cause several forms of pollution. Packed tightly, fish rub against each other and the sides of their cages, damaging their fins and tails and becoming sickened with various diseases and infections.

However, fish tend also to be animals that aggregate into large schools at high density. Most successful aquaculture species are schooling species, which do not have social problems at high density. Aquaculturists tend to feel that operating a rearing system above its design capacity or above the social density limit of the fish will result in decreased growth rate and FCR (food conversion ratio - kg dry feed/kg of fish produced), which will result in increased cost and risk of health problems along with a decrease in profits. Stressing the animals is not desirable, but the concept of and measurement of stress must be viewed from the perspective of the animal using the scientific method.

Some species of sea lice have been noted to target farmed coho and Atlantic salmon Such parasites have been shown to have an effect on nearby wild fish. One place that has garnered international media attention is British Columbia's Broughton Archipelago. There, juvenile wild salmon must "run a gauntlet" of large fish farms located off-shore near river outlets before making their way to sea. It is alleged that the farms cause such severe sea lice infestations that one study predicted a 99% collapse in the wild salmon population in another four years. This claim, however, has been criticized by numerous scientists who question the correlation between increased fish farming and increases in sea lice infestation among wild salmon.

Because of parasite problems, some aquaculture operators frequently use strong antibiotic drugs to keep the fish alive (but many fish still die prematurely at rates of up to 30% . In some cases, these drugs have entered the environment. Additionally, the residual presence of these drugs in human food products has become controversial. Use of antibiotics in food production is thought to increase the prevalence of antibiotic resistance in human diseases. The use of antibiotic drugs in aquaculture has decreased considerably in the last decade. Vaccinations and other techniques have virtually eliminated the need for antibiotics.

The lice and pathogen problems of the 1990s facilitated the development of current treatment methods for sea lice and pathogens. These developments reduced the stress from parasite/ pathogen problems. However, being in an ocean environment, the transfer of disease organisms from the wild fish to the aquaculture fish is an ever-present risk factor.

The very large number of fish kept long-term in a single location produces a significant amount of condensed feces, often contaminated with drugs, which again affect local waterways. However, these effects are very local to the actual fish farm site and are minimal to non-measurable in high current sites.

Other potential problems faced by aquaculturists are the obtaining of various permits and water-use rights, profitability, concerns about invasive species and genetic engineering depending on what species are involved, and interaction with the United Nations Convention on the Law of the Sea.

Recirculating Aquaculture System

An alternative to open ocean cage aquaculture, one in which the risk of environmental damage is substantially eliminated is through the use of a recirculating aquaculture system (RAS). A RAS is a series of culture tanks and filters where water is continuously recycled. To prevent the deterioration of water quality, the water is treated mechanically through the removal of particulate matter and biologically through the conversion of harmful accumulated chemicals into nontoxic ones.

Other treatments such as UV sterilization, ozonation, and oxygen injection are also utilized to maintain optimal water quality. Through this system, many of the environmental drawbacks of aquaculture are minimized including escaped fish, water usage, and the introduction of harmful pollutants. The practices also increase efficiency of feed utilisation and growth by providing optimal water quality parameters.

One of the drawbacks to recirculating aquaculture systems is water exchange. However, the rate of water exchange can be reduced through aquaponics, such as the incorporation of hydroponically grown plants (Corpron and Armstrong, 1983) and denitrification (Klas et al., 2006). Both methods reduce the amount of nitrate in the water, and can potentially eliminate the need for water exchanges, closing the aquaculture system from the environment. The amount of interaction between the aquaculture system and the environment can be measured through the cumulative feed burden (CFB kg/M3), which measures the amount of feed that goes into the RAS relative to the amount of water and waste discharged.

Because of its high capital and operating costs, RAS has generally been restricted to practices such as broodstock maturation, larval rearing, fingerling production, research animal production, SPF (specific pathogen free) animal production, and caviar and ornamental fish production. Although the use of RAS for other species is considered by many aquaculturalists to be impractical, there has been some limited successful implementation of this with high value product such as barramundi, sturgeon and live tilapia in the US.

Fish Hatchery

Fish hatcheries are used to cultivate and breed a large number of fish in an enclosed environment.

These are typically involve a lot of manual labour. A hatchery worker will take a female fish, release her eggs (stripping), and then externally add the male fish's sperm (milt), mix them and allow them to fertilize and incubate undisturbed, where there is less risk of disease or predation. They can immediately dispose of any unfertilized eggs. What happens next depends on the purpose of the Hatchery. Fish farms use Hatcheries to cultivate fish to sell for food, or ornamental purposes, eliminating the need to find the fish in the wild and even providing some species outside of their natural season. They raise the fish until they are ready to be eaten or sold to aquarium stores.

Other Uses

Other Hatcheries release the juvenile fish into a river, lake or the ocean to support commercial, tribal, or recreational fishing or to supplement the natural numbers of threatened or endangered species, a practice known as fish stocking. Some fish Hatcheries are used to mitigate the effects of development, such as construction of a dam, hydroelectric plant or water diversion. In the United States and Canada, these hatcheries usually raise anadromous fish that are unable to migrate due to the obstruction, particularly salmon and steelhead. In 1889 a cod fish hatchery was erected on an island belonging to Newfoundland and Labrador. It was the largest hatchery in the world at that time and the first in North America. The ornamental fish industry uses fish hatcheries to produce fish for the aquarium fish trade, this has helped to limit the over harvesting of native fish populations both in fresh and salt water ecosystems.

Originally devised to mitigate for fish production lost through development and supply the demand for fishing from an expanding human population, fish hatcheries have been causing problems by producing poor quality or genetically inferior fish. Several researchers have raised concerns about hatchery fish potentially breeding with wild fish. Hatchery fish may in some cases compete with wild fish. There is lively debate among the scientific community regarding the risks and benefits of hatchery programs. Proving negative (or positive) effects of hatchery programs on wild fish is challenging due to numerous other environmental and anthropogenic factors that simultaneously affect fish. In the United States and Canada, there have been several salmon and steelhead hatchery reform projects intended to reduce the possibility of negative impacts from hatchery programs. Most salmon and steelhead hatcheries are managed better and follow up to date management practices to ensure any risks are minimized.

Salmon

Salmon is the common name for several species of fish of the family Salmonidae. Several other fish in the family are called trout. Salmon live in both the Atlantic and Pacific Oceans, as well as the Great Lakes and other land locked lakes.

Typically, salmon are anadromous: they are born in fresh water, migrate to the ocean, then return to fresh water to reproduce. However, there are rare species that can only survive in fresh water habitats. This is most likely due to the domestication of these certain species of Salmon. Folklore has it that the fish return to the exact spot where they were born to spawn.

The salmon has long been at the heart of the culture and livelihood of coastal dwellers. Most peoples of the Northern Pacific shore had a ceremony to honor the first return of the year. For many centuries, people caught salmon as they swam upriver to spawn. A famous spearfishing site on the Columbia River at Celilo Falls was inundated after great dams were built on the river. The Ainu, of northern Japan, taught dogs how to catch salmon as they returned to their breeding grounds *en masse*. Now, salmon are caught in bays and near shore.

Salmon population levels are of concern in the Atlantic and in some parts of the Pacific but in Alaska stocks are still abundant. Fish farming is outlawed [and the State of Alaska's fisheries management system is viewed as the global leader in the management of wild, sustainable fish stocks.[*citation needed*] The most important Alaska Salmon sustainable wild fisheries are located near the Kenai River, Copper River, and in Bristol Bay. In Canada, returning Skeena River wild salmon support commercial, subsistence and recreational fisheries as well as the area's diverse wildlife on the coast and around communities hundreds of miles inland in the watershed. The Columbia River salmon population is now less than 3% of what it was when Lewis and Clark arrived at the river. Both Atlantic and Pacific Salmon are important to recreational fishing around the world.

Life Cycle of Salmon

Salmon fry hatching - the larva has grown around the remains of the yolk - visible are the arteries spinning around the yolk and little oildrops, also the gut, the spine, the main caudal blood vessel, the bladder and the arcs of the gills.

In Alaska, the crossing-over to other streams allows salmon to populate new streams, such as those that emerge as a glacier retreats. The precise method salmon use to navigate has not been entirely established, though their keen sense of smell is involved. In all species of Pacific salmon, the mature individuals die within a few days or weeks of spawning, a trait known as semelparity. However, even in those species of salmon that may survive to spawn more than once (iteroparity), post-spawning mortality is quite high (perhaps as high as 40 to 50%.)

In order to lay her roe, the female salmon uses her dorsal fin to excavate a shallow depression, called a *redd*. The redd may sometimes contain 5,000 eggs covering 30 square feet (2.8 m2). he eggs usually range from orange to red in color. One or more males will approach the female in her redd, depositing his sperm, or milt, over the roe The female then covers the eggs by disturbing the gravel at the upstream edge of the depression before moving on to make another redd. The female will make as many as 7 redds before her supply of eggs is exhausted. The salmon then die within a few days of spawning.

The eggs will hatch into *alevin* or *sac fry*. The fry quickly develop into *parr* with camouflaging vertical stripes. The parr stay for one to three years in their natal stream before becoming *smolts* which are distinguished by their bright silvery colour with scales that are easily rubbed off. It is estimated that only 10% of all salmon eggs survive long enough to reach this stages. The smolt body chemistry changes, allowing them to live in salt water. Smolts spend a portion of their out-migration time in brackish water, where their body chemistry becomes accustomed to osmoregulation in the ocean.

The salmon spend about one to five years (depending on the species) in the open ocean where they will become sexually mature. The adult salmon returns primarily to its natal stream to spawn. When fish return for the first time they are called *whitling* in the UK and *grilse* or *peel* in Ireland. Prior to spawning, depending on the species, the salmon undergoes changes. They may grow a hump, develop canine teeth, develop a *kype* (a pronounced curvature of the jaws in male salmon). All will change from the silvery blue of a fresh run fish from the sea to a darker color. Condition tends to deteriorate the longer the fish remain in freshwater, and they then deteriorate further after they spawn becoming known as *kelts*. Salmon can make amazing journeys, sometimes moving hundreds of miles upstream against strong currents and rapids to reproduce. Chinook and sockeye salmon from central Idaho, for example, travel over 900 miles (1,400 km) and climb nearly 7,000 feet (2,100 m) from the Pacific ocean as they return to spawn.

Each year, the fish experiences a period of rapid growth, often in summer, and one of slower growth, normally in winter. This results in rings (annuli) analogous to the growth rings visible in a tree trunk. Freshwater growth shows as densely crowded rings, sea growth as widely spaced rings; spawning is marked by significant erosion as body mass is converted into eggs and milt.

Freshwater streams and estuaries provide important habitat for many salmon species. They feed on terrestrial and aquatic insects, amphipods, and other crustaceans while young, and primarily on other fish when older. Eggs are laid in deeper water with larger gravel, and need cool water and good water flow (to supply oxygen) to the developing embryos. Mortality of salmon in the early life stages is usually high due to natural predation and human induced changes in habitat, such as siltation, high water temperatures, low oxygen conditions, loss of stream cover, and reductions in river flow. Estuaries and their associated wetlands provide vital nursery areas for the salmon prior to their departure to the open ocean. Wetlands not only help buffer the estuary from silt and pollutants, but also provide important feeding and hiding areas.

Salmon as Food

Salmon is a popular food. Consuming salmon is considered to be reasonably healthy due to the fish's high protein, high Omega-3 fatty acids, and high vitamin D content. Salmon is also a source of cholesterol, ranging 23–214 mg/100g depending on the species. According to reports in the *Science* journal, however, farmed salmon may contain high levels of dioxins. PCB (polychlorinated biphenyl) levels may be up to eight times higher in farmed salmon than in wild salmon. Omega-3 content may also be lower than in wild caught individuals, and in a different proportion to what is found naturally. Omega 3 comes in three types, ALA, DHA and EPA; wild salmon has traditionally been an important source of DHA and EPA, which are important for brain function and structure, among other things. This means that if the farmed salmon is fed on a meal which is partially grain then the amount of Omega 3 it contains will be present as ALA (alpha-linolenic acid). The body can itself convert ALA Omega 3 into DHA and EPA, but at a very inefficient rate (2–15%). Nonetheless, according to a 2006 study published in the Journal of the American Medical Association, the benefits of eating even farmed salmon still outweigh any risks imposed by contaminants Type of Omega 3 present may not be a factor for other important health functions. A simple rule of thumb is that the vast majority of Atlantic salmon available on the world market are farmed (greater than 99%), whereas the majority of Pacific salmon are wild-caught (greater than 80%). Farmed salmon outnumber wild salmon 85 to 1.

Salmon flesh is generally orange to red in colour, although there are some examples of white fleshed wild salmon. The natural colour of salmon results from carotenoid pigments, largely astaxanthin (E161j), in the flesh. Wild salmon get these carotenoids from eating krill and other tiny shellfish. Because consumers have shown a reluctance to purchase white fleshed salmon, astaxanthin, and very minutely canthaxanthin (E161g), are added as artificial colorants to the feed of farmed salmon because prepared diets do not naturally contain these pigments. In most cases the astaxanthin is made chemically; alternatively it is extracted from shrimp flour. Another possibility is the use of dried red yeast, which provides the same pigment. However, synthetic mixtures are the least expensive option. Astaxanthin is a potent antioxidant that stimulates the development of healthy fish nervous systems and that enhances the fish's fertility and growth rate. Research has revealed canthaxanthin may have negative effects on the human eye, accumulating in the retina at high levels of consumption Today the concentration of carotenoids (mainly canthaxanthin and astaxanthin) exceeds 8 mg/kg of flesh and all fish producers try to reach a level that represents a value of 16 on the "Roche Color Card", a colour card used to show how pink the fish will appear at specific doses. This scale is specific for measuring the pink colour due to astaxanthin and is not for the orange hue obtained with canthaxanthin. The development of processing and storage operations, which can be detrimental on canthaxanthin flesh concentration, has led to an increased quantity of pigments added to the diet to compensate for the degrading effects of the processing. In wild fish, carotenoid levels of up to 20–25 mg are present, but levels of canthaxanthin are, in contrast, minor.

Canned salmon in the U.S. is usually wild Pacific catch, though some farmed salmon is available in canned form. Smoked salmon is another popular preparation method, and can either be hot or cold smoked. Lox can refer either to cold smoked salmon or to salmon cured in a brine solution (also called gravlax). Traditional canned salmon includes some skin (which is harmless) and bone (which adds calcium). Skinless and boneless canned salmon is also available.

Raw salmon flesh may contain *Anisakis* nematodes, marine parasites that cause Anisakiasis. Before the availability of refrigeration, the Japanese did not consume raw salmon. Salmon and salmon roe have only recently come into use in making sashimi (raw fish) and sushi

Environmental Pressures

Many wild Salmon stocks have seen a marked decline in recent decades, especially north Atlantic populations which spawn in western European and eastern Canadian waters, and wild salmon of the Snake and Columbia River systems in the Northwest USA. The causes of these declines likely include a number of factors, among them:

- Disease transfer from open net cage salmon farming, especially sea lice. The European Commission (2002) concluded "The reduction of wild salmonid abundance is also linked to other factors but there is more and more scientific evidence establishing a direct link between the number of lice-infested wild fish and the presence of cages in the same estuary." It is reported that wild salmon on the west coast of Canada are being driven to extinction by sea lice from nearby salmon farms.
- For Atlantic salmon smolts, it takes as few as eight sea lice to kill the fish. On the Pacific Coast where the smolt are much smaller, only one or two are needed. In the Atlantic, sea lice have been a proven factor in both Norwegian and Scottish salmon. In the Western Atlantic there has been little research at sea, but sea lice numbers in the period post-2000 do not appear to be a significant factor in the critical decline of endangered inner Bay of Fundy salmon. The situation may have been different in the 1980s and 1990s, but we are unlikely ever to know the true facts on that.
- Overfishing in general but especially commercial netting in the Faroes and Greenland.
- Ocean and river warming which can delay spawning and accelerate transition to smolting.

- Ulcerative dermal necrosis (UDN) infections of the 1970s and 1980s which severely affected adult salmon in freshwater rivers.
- Loss of suitable freshwater habitat, especially degradation of stream pools and reduction of suitable material for the excavation of redds. Historically stream pools were, to a large extent, created by beavers. With the extirpation of the beaver, the nurturing function of these ponds was lost.
- Reduction of the retention of the nutrients brought by the returning adult salmon in stream pools. Without stream pools, dead adult salmon tend to be washed straight back down the streams and rivers.
- The construction of dams, weirs, barriers and other "flood prevention" measures, which bring severe adverse impacts to river habitat and on the accessibility of those habitats to salmon. This is particularly true in the northwest USA, where large numbers of dams have been built in many river systems, including over 400 in the Columbia River Basin.
- Loss of invertebrate diversity and population density in rivers because of modern farming methods and various sources of pollution, thus reducing food availability.
- Reduction in freshwater base flow in rivers and disruption of seasonal flows, because of diversions and extractions, hydroelectric power generation, irrigation schemes, and slackwater reservoirs, which inhibit normal migratory processes and increase predation for salmon.

There are efforts to relieve this situation. As such, several governments and NGOs are sharing in research and habitat restoration efforts.

- In the western Atlantic, the Atlantic Salmon Federation has developed a major sonic tracking technology program to understand the high at-sea mortality since the early 1990s. Ocean arrays are deployed across the Baies des Chaleurs and between Newfoundland and Labrador at the Strait of Belle Isle. Salmon have now been tracked half way from rivers like the Restigouche to Greenland feeding grounds.

Now the first line of the Ocean Tracking Network initiative is installed by DFO and Dalhousie University of Halifax from Halifax to the edge of the continental shelf. First results include Atlantic salmon travelling from the Penobscot River in Maine, the "anchor river" for US Atlantic salmon populations.

Results overall are showing that estuary problems exist for some rivers, but issues involving feeding grounds at sea are impacting populations as well. In 2008 returns were markedly improved for Atlantic salmon on both sides of the Atlantic Ocean, but no one knows if this is a temporary improvement or sign of a trend.

Salmon and Beavers

Beavers' ponds may provide critical habitat for juvenile salmon. An example of this was seen in the years following 1818 in the Columbia River Basin. In 1818, the British government made an agreement with the U.S. government to allow U.S. citizens access to the Columbia catchment (see Treaty of 1818). At the time, the Hudson's Bay Company sent word to trappers to extirpate all furbearers from the area in an effort to make the area less attractive. In response to the elimination of beavers from large parts of the river system, salmon runs plummeted, even in the absence of many of the factors usually associated with the demise of salmon runs. Salmon recruitment can be effected by beavers' dams because dams can:

- Slow the rate at which nutrients are flushed from the system; nutrients provided by adult salmon dying throughout the fall and winter remain available in the spring to newly-hatched juveniles.
- Provide deeper water pools where young salmon can avoid avian predators.
- Increase productivity through photosynthesis and by enhancing the conversion efficiency of the cellulose-powered detritus cycle.
- Create low-energy environments where juvenile salmon put the food they ingest into growth rather than into fighting currents.

- Increase structural complexity with many physical niches where salmon can avoid predators.

Beavers' dams are able to nurture salmon juveniles in Estuarine tidal marshes where the salinity is less than 10ppm. Beavers build small dams of generally less than 2 feet (0.61 m) high in channels in the Myrtle zone. These dams can be overtopped at high tide and hold water at low tide. This provides refuges for juvenile salmon so they don't have to swim into large channels where they are subject to predation.

Aquaculture

Almon aquaculture is the major economic contributor to the world production of farmed fin-fish, representing over $1 billion US annually. Other commonly cultured fish species include: tilapia, catfish, sea bass, carp, bream, and trout. Salmon farming is very big in Chile, Norway, Scotland, Canada and the Faroe Islands, and is the source for most salmon consumed in America and Europe. Atlantic salmon are also, in very small volumes, farmed in Russia, Tasmania, Australia.

Salmon are carnivorous and are currently fed a meal produced from catching other wild fish and other marine organisms. Consequently, as the number of farmed salmon increase, so does the demand for other fish to feed the salmon. Work continues on substituting vegetable proteins for animal proteins in the salmon diet. Unfortunately though, this substitution results in lower levels of the highly valued Omega-3 content in the farmed product. Intensive salmon farming now uses open net cages which have low production costs but have the drawback of allowing disease and sea lice to spread to local wild salmon stocks.

On a dry-dry basis, it takes 2-4 kg of wild caught fish to produce one kg of salmon Salmon farms (feed lots actually, as there is no farming involved) introduce levels of untreated sewage into the ocean that has already been outlawed for sea side communities. This detritus is thought to contribute to toxic algal blooms and also has negative affects on local benthic communities.

Another form of salmon production, which is safer but less controllable, is to raise salmon in hatcheries until they are old enough to become independent. They are then released into rivers, often in an attempt to increase the salmon population. This practice was very common in countries like Sweden before the Norwegians developed salmon farming, but is seldom done by private companies, as anyone may catch the salmon when they return to spawn, limiting a company's chances of benefiting financially from their investment. Because of this, the method has mainly been used by various public authorities as a way of artificially increasing salmon populations in situations where they have declined due to overharvest, construction of dams, and habitat destruction or disruption. Unfortunately, there can be negative consequences to this sort of population manipulation, including genetic "dilution" of the wild stocks, and many jurisdictions are now beginning to discourage supplemental fish planting in favour of harvest controls and habitat improvement and protection. A variant method of fish stocking, called ocean ranching, is under development in Alaska. There, the young salmon are released into the ocean far from any wild salmon streams. When it is time for them to spawn, they return to where they were released where fishermen can then catch them.

An alternative method to hatcheries is to use spawning channels. These are artificial streams, usually parallel to an existing stream with cement or rip-rap sides and gravel bottoms. Water from the adjacent stream is piped into the top of the channel, sometimes via a header pond to settle out sediment. Spawning success is often much better in channels than in adjacent streams due to the control of floods which in some years can wash out the natural redds. Because of the lack of floods, spawning channels must sometimes be cleaned out to remove accumulated sediment. The same floods which destroy natural redds also clean them out. Spawning channels preserve the natural selection of natural streams as there is no temptation, as in hatcheries, to use propholactic chemicals to control diseases.

Farm raised salmon are fed the carotenoids astaxanthin and canthaxanthin, so that their flesh color matches wild salmon.

Diseases and Parasites Affecting Wild Salmon

According to Canadian biologist Dr. Dorothy Kieser, protozoan parasite Henneguya salminicola is commonly found in the flesh of salmonids. It has been recorded in the field samples of salmon returning to Queen Charlotte Island streams. The fish responds by walling off the parasitic infection into a number of cysts that contain milky fluid. This fluid is an accumulation of a large number of parasites.

Henneguya and other parasites in the myxosporean group have a complex lifecycle where the salmon is one of two hosts. The fish releases the spores after spawning. In the Henneguya case, the spores enter a second host, most likely an invertebrate, in the spawning stream. When juvenile salmon out-migrate to the Pacific Ocean, the second host releases a stage infective to salmon. The parasite is then carried in the salmon until the next spawning cycle. The myxosporean parasite that causes whirling disease in trout, has a similar lifecycle. However, as opposed to whirling disease, the Henneguya infestation does not appear to cause disease in the host salmon - even heavily infected fish tend to return to spawn successfully.

According to Dr. Kieser, a lot of work on Henneguya salminicola was done by scientists at the Pacific Biological Station in Nanaimo in the mid-1980, in particular, an overview report which states that "the fish that have the longest fresh water residence time as juveniles have the most noticeable infections. Hence in order of prevalence coho are most infected followed by sockeye, chinook, chum and pink." As well, the report says that, at the time the studies were conducted, stocks from the middle and upper reaches of large river systems in British Columbia such as Fraser, Skeena, Nass and from mainland coastal streams in the southern half of B.C. "are more likely to have a low prevalence of infection." The report also states "It should be stressed that Henneguya, economically deleterious though it is, is harmless from the view of public health. It is strictly a fish parasite that cannot live in or affect warm blooded animals, including man".

According to Klaus Schallie, Molluscan Shellfish Program Specialist with the Canadian Food Inspection Agency, "Henneguya salminicola is found in southern B.C. also and in all species of salmon. I have previously examined smoked chum salmon sides that were riddled with cysts and some sockeye runs in Barkley Sound (southern B.C., west coast of Vancouver Island) are noted for their high incidence of infestation."

Freshwater Prawn Farm

A *freshwater prawn farm* is an aquaculture business designed to raise and produce freshwater prawn or shrimp1 for human consumption. Freshwater prawn farming shares many characteristics with, and many of the same problems as, marine shrimp farming. Unique problems are introduced by the developmental life cycle of the main species (the giant river prawn, *Macrobrachium rosenbergii*).

The global annual production of freshwater prawns (excluding crayfish and crabs) in 2003 was about 280,000 tons, of which China produced some 180,000 tons, followed by India and Thailand with some 35,000 tons each. Additionally, China produced about 370,000 tons of Chinese river crab (*Eriocheir sinensis*).

Species

All farmed freshwater prawns today belong to the genus *Macrobrachium*. Until 2000, the only species farmed was the Giant river prawn (*Macrobrachium rosenbergii*, also known as the Malaysian prawn). Since then, China has begun farming the Oriental river prawn (*M. nipponense*) in large quantities, and India farms a small amount of monsoon river prawn (*M. malcolmsonii*). In 2003, these three species accounted for all farmed freshwater prawns, about two thirds *M. rosenbergii* and one third *M. nipponense*.

There are about 200 species in the genus *Macrobrachium*. They occur throughout the tropics and subtropics on all continents except Europe.

Biology of Macrobrachium rosenbergii

Giant river prawns live in turbid freshwater, but their larval stages require brackish water to survive. Males can reach a body size of 32 cm;females grow to 25 cm. In mating, the male deposits spermatophores on the underside of the female's thorax, between the walking legs. The female then extrudes eggs, which pass through the spermatophores. The female carries the fertilized eggs with her until they hatch; the time may vary, but is generally less than three weeks. A large female may lay up to 100,000 eggs.

From these eggs hatch zoeae, the first larval stage of crustaceans. They go through several larval stages before metamorphosing into postlarvae, at which stage they are about 8 mm long and have all the characteristics of adults. This metamorphosis usually takes place about 32 to 35 days after hatching. These postlarvae then migrate back into freshwater.

There are three different morphotypes of males. The first stage is called "small male" (SM); this smallest stage has short, nearly translucent claws. If conditions allow, small males grow and metamorphose into "orange claws" (OC), which have large orange claws on their second chelipeds, which may have a length of 0.8 to 1.4 their body size. OC males later may transform into the third and final stage, the "blue claw" (BC) males. These have blue claws, and their second chelipeds may become twice as long as their body

Male *M. rosenbergii* have a strict hierarchy: the territorial BC males dominate the OCs, which in turn dominate the SMs. The presence of BC males inhibts the growth of SMs and delays the metamorphosis of OCs into BCs; an OC will keep growing until it is larger than the largest BC male in its neighbourhood before transforming. All three male stages are sexually active though, and females who have undergone their pre-mating molt will cooperate with any male to reproduce. BC males protect the female until their shell has hardened, OCs and SMs show no such behaviour.

Technology

Giant River Prawns have been farmed using traditional methods in south-east Asia for a long time. First experiments with artificial breeding cultures of *M. rosenbergii* were done in the early 1960s in Malaysia, where it was discovered that the larvae needed brackish water for survival. Industrial-scale rearing processes were perfected in the early 1970s in Hawaii, and spread then first to Taiwan and Thailand and then to other countries.

The technologies used in freshwater prawn farming are basically the same as in marine shrimp farming. hatcheries produce postlarvae, which then are grown and acclimated in nurseries before being transferred into growout ponds, where the prawns are then fed and grown until they reach marketable size. Harvesting is done by either draining the pond and collecting the animals ("batch" harvesting) or by fishing the prawns out of the pond using nets (continuous operation).

Due to the aggressive nature of *M. rosenbergii* and the hierarchy between males, stocking densities are much lower than in penaeid shrimp farms. Intensive farming is not possible due to the increased level of cannibalism, so all farms are either stocked semi-intensively (4 to 20 postlarvae per square metre) or, in extensive farms, at even lower densities (1 to 4/m^2). The management of the growout ponds must take into account the growth characteristics of *M. rosenbergii*: the presence of blue-claw males inhibits the growth of small males, and delays the metamorphosis of OC males into blue-claws. Some farms fish off the largest prawns from the pond using seines to ensure a healthy composition of the pond's population, designed to optimize the yield, even if they employ batch harvesting. The heterogeneous individual growth of *M. rosenbergii* makes growth control necessary even if a pond is stocked newly, starting from scratch: some animals will grow faster than others and become dominant BCs, shunting the growth of other individuals.

The FAO considers the ecological impact of freshwater prawn farming to be less severe than in shrimp farming. The prawns are cultured at much lower densities, meaning less concentrated waste products and a lesser danger of the ponds becoming breeding places for diseases. The growout ponds do not salinate agricultural land, as do those of inland marine shrimp farms. Freshwater prawn farms do not endanger mangroves, and are better amenable to small-scale businesses run by a family However, like marine farmed shrimp, *M. rosenbergii* is also susceptible to a variety of viral or bacterial diseases, ncluding the White Tail Disease also called "White Muscle Disease".

Economics

The global annual production of freshwater prawns in 2003 was about 280,000 tonnes, of which China produced some 180,000 tonnes, followed by India and Thailand with some 35,000 tonnes each. Other major producer countries are Taiwan, Bangladesh, and Vietnam. In the United States, there are only a few hundred small farms for *M. rosenbergii* with an overall production of just about 50 tonnes in 2003. The U.S. is, though, the largest producer of farmed crayfish. In 2003, U.S. farms produced 33,500 tonnes of red swamp crawfish (*Procambarus clarkii*), a crayfish species native to North America.

Oyster farming is an aquaculture (or mariculture) practice in which oysters are raised for human consumption. Oyster farming most likely developed in tandem with pearl farming, a similar practice in which oysters are farmed for the purpose of developing pearls. It has been practiced in one form or another since the Ancient Romans cultured oysters in Great Britain and transported them to Italy. The French oyster industry has relied on aquacultured oysters since the late 18th century.

Commonly farmed food oysters include the Eastern oyster *Crassostrea virginica* , the Pacific oyster *Crassostrea gigas,* Belon oyster *Ostrea edulis,* the Sydney rock oyster *Saccostrea glomerata,* and the Southern mud oyster *Ostrea angasi.* Oysters naturally grow in estuarine bodies of brackish water. When farmed the temperature and salinity of the water are controlled (or at least monitored) so as to induce spawning and fertilization, as well as to speed the rate of maturation - which can take several years.

Three methods of cultivation are commonly used. In each case oysters are cultivated to the size of "spat," the point at which they attach themselves to a substrate. The substrate is known as a "culch" or "cultch". The loose spat may be allowed to mature further to form "seed" oysters with small shells. In either case (spat or seed stage) they are then set out to mature. The maturation technique is where the cultivation method choice is made.

In one method the spat or seed oysters are distributed over existing oyster beds and left to mature naturally. Such oysters will then be collected using the methods for fishing wild oysters, such as dredging.

In the second method the spat or seed may be put in racks, bags, or cages which are held above the bottom. Oysters cultivated in this manner may be harvested by lifting the bags or rack to the surface and removing mature oysters, or simply retrieving the larger oysters when the enclosure is exposed at low tide. The latter method may avoid losses to some predators but is more expensive.

In the third method the spat or seed are placed in a culch within an artificial maturation tank. The maturation tank may be fed with water that has been especially prepared for the purpose of accelerating the growth rate of the oysters. In particular the temperature and salinity of the water may be altered somewhat from nearby ocean water. The carbonate minerals calcite and aragonite in the water may help oysters develop their shells faster and may also be included in the water processing prior to introduction to the tanks. This latter cultivation technique may be the least susceptable to predators and poaching but is the most expensive to build and to operate The Pacific oyster *C. gigas* is the species most commonly used with this type of farming.

Oyster predators include starfish, oyster drill snails, stingrays, Florida stone crabs, birds such as oystercatchers and gulls, as well as humans. Diseases that can affect either farmed *C. virginica* or *C. gigas* oysters include *Perkinsus marinus* (Dermo) and *Haplosporidium nelsoni* (MSX). However, *C. viginicus* are much more susceptible to Dermo or MSX infections than are the *C. gigas* species of oyster Pathogens of *O. edulis* oysters include *Marteilia refringens* and *Bonamia ostrea* In the north Atlantic Ocean, oyster crabs may live in an endosymbiotic commensal relationship within a host oyster. Since oyster crabs are considered a food delicacy they may not be removed from young farmed oysters, as they can themselves be harvested for sale.

Trout

Trout is the common name given to a number of species of freshwater fish belonging to the Salmonidae family.

Species

All fish called trout are members of the subfamily Salmonidae. The name is commonly used for species in three of the seven genera in the sub-family: *Salmo,*Atlantic species; *Salvelinus,*which includes fish also sometimes called *char* or *charr*. Pacific species; *Oncorhynchus,* Fish referred to as trout include:

Genus	*Salmo*
	Adriatic trout, *Salmo obtusirostris*
	Brown trout, *Salmo trutta*
	Flathead trout, *Salmo platycephalus*
	Marmorata, Soca River trout or Soca trout - *Salmo trutta marmoratus*
	Ohrid trout, *Salmo letnica*
	Sevan trout, *Salmo ischchan*
Genus	*Oncorhynchus*
	Apache trout, *Oncorhynchus Apache*
	Eskimo trout, *Oncorhynchus inupiat* [*verification needed*]
	Seema, *Oncorhynchus masou*
	Cutthroat trout, *Oncorhynchus clarki*

The cutthroat trout has 14 recognized subspecies (depending on your sources), such as the Lahontan cutthroat trout, *Oncorhynchus clarki henshawi,* Bonneville cutthroat trout, *Oncorhynchus clarki utah,* Colorado River cutthroat trout, Yellowstone cutthroat trout.

Gila trout, *Oncorhynchus gilae*
Golden trout, *Oncorhynchus aguabonita*
Rainbow trout, *Oncorhynchus mykiss*
Mexican Golden Trout, *Oncorhynchus chrysogaster* and as many as eight other species or sub-species in northwest Mexico, not yet formally named.

Genus	*Salvelinus* (Char)
	Arctic char, *Salvelinus alpinus*
	Aurora trout, *Salvelinus fontinalis timagamiensis*
	Brook trout, *Salvelinus fontinalis*
	Bull trout, *Salvelinus confluentus*
	Dolly Varden trout, *Salvelinus malma*
	Lake trout, *Salvelinus namaycush*
	Silver trout, † *Salvelinus fontinalis agassizi* (extinct)

Habitat

Trout are usually found in cool (50-60°F, 10-15°C), clear streams and lakes, although many of the species have anadromous strains as well. Young trout are referred to as troutlet or troutling. They are distributed naturally throughout North America, northern Asia and Europe. Several species of trout were introduced to Australia and New Zealand by amateur fishing enthusiasts in the 19th century, effectively displacing and endangering several upland native fish species. The introduced species included brown trout from England and rainbow trout from California. The rainbow trout were a steelhead strain, generally accepted as coming from Sonoma Creek. The rainbow trout of New Zealand still show the steelhead tendency to run up rivers in winter to spawn The speckled trout, found in the Gulf of Mexico and other places in the United States, is not in fact a trout at all, but a member of the drum family.

Anatomy

Trout that live in different environments can have dramatically different colorations and patterns. Mostly, these colors and patterns form as camouflage, based on the surroundings, and will change as the fish moves to different habitats. Trout in, or newly returned from the sea, can look very silvery, while the same "genetic" fish living in a small stream or in an alpine lake could have pronounced markings and more vivid coloration; it is also possible that in some species this signifies that they are ready to mate. It is virtually impossible to define a particular color pattern as belonging to a specific breed; however, in general, wild fish are claimed to have more vivid colors and patterns.

Trout have fins entirely without spines, and all of them have a small adipose (fatty) fin along the back, near the tail. There are many species, and even more populations that are isolated from each other and morphologically different. However, since many of these distinct populations show no significant genetic differences, what may appear to be a large number of species is considered a much smaller number of distinct species by most ichthyologists. The trout found in the eastern United States are a good example of this. The brook trout, the aurora trout, and the (extinct) silver trout all have physical characteristics and colorations that distinguish them, yet genetic analysis shows that they are one species, *Salvelinus fontinalis*.

Lake trout (*Salvelinus namaycush*), like brook trout, actually belong to the char genus. Lake trout inhabit many of the larger lakes in North America, and live much longer than rainbow trout, which have an average maximum lifespan of 7 years. Lake trout can live many decades, and can grow to more than 30 kilograms

River Fishing

Understanding how moving water shapes the stream channel will improve your chances of finding trout. In most streams, the current creates a Riffle-Run-Pool pattern that repeats itself over and over. A deep pool may hold a big brown trout, but rainbows and smaller browns are likely found in runs. Riffles are where you will find small trout, called troutlet, during the day and larger trout crowding in during morning and evening feeding periods.

- Riffles have a fast current and shallow water. This gives way to a bottom of gravel, rubble or boulder. Riffles are morning and evening feeding areas. Trout usually spawn just above or below riffles, but may spawn right in them.
- Runs are deeper than riffles with a moderate current and are found between riffles and pools. The bottom is made up of small gravel or rubble. These hot spots hold trout almost anytime, if there is sufficient cover.
- Pools are smoother and look darker than the other areas of the stream. The deep, slow-moving water generally has a

bottom of silt, sand, or small gravel. Pools make good midday resting spots for medium to large trout.

Trout Consumption

As a group, trout are somewhat bony, but the flesh is generally considered to be appetizing. Additionally, they provide a good fight when caught with a hook and line, and are sought after recreationally. Because of their popularity, trout are often raised on fish farms and planted into heavily fished waters, in an effort to mask the effects of overfishing. While they can be caught with a normal rod and reel, fly fishing is a distinctive method developed primarily for trout, and now extended to other species. Farmed trout and char are also sold commercially as food fish.

8

Seafood

Introduction

Seafood is any sea animal or seaweed that is served as food, or is suitable for eating, particularly saltwater animals, such as fish and shellfish (including mollusks and crustaceans). By extension, in North America although not generally in the United Kingdom, the term *seafood* is also loosely applied to similar edible animals from fresh water. Edible seaweeds are also seafood, and are widely eaten around the world. See the category of sea vegetables. *The harvesting of seafood* is known as fishing and the cultivation of seafood is known as aquaculture, mariculture, or in the case of fish, fish farming. Seafood is an important source of protein in many diets around the world, especially in coastal areas. Research into population trends of various species of seafood is pointing to a global collapse of seafood species by 2048. Such a collapse would occur due to pollution and overfishing, threatening oceanic ecosystems, according to some researchers.

A major international scientific study released in November 2006 in the journal *Science* found that about one-third of all fishing stocks worldwide have collapsed (with a collapse being defined as a decline to less than 10% of their maximum observed abundance), and that if current trends continue all fish stocks worldwide will collapse within fifty years. The FAO State of World Fisheries and Aquaculture 2004 report estimates that in

2003, of the main fish stocks or groups of resources for which assessment information is available, "approximately one-quarter were overexploited, depleted or recovering from depletion (16%, 7% and 1% respectively) and needed rebuilding." Advocacy organizations such as the National Fisheries Institute, however, disagree with such findings and assert that currently observed declines in fish population are due to natural fluctuations and that enhanced technologies will eventually alleviate whatever impact humanity is having on oceanic life

Fish as Food

Fish as food describes the edible parts of freshwater and saltwater-dwelling, cold-blooded vertebrates with gills. Shellfish, such as mollusks and crustaceans, are other edible water-dwelling animals that fall into the broadest category of fish.

Fish is consumed as food all over the world; with other seafoods, it provides the world's prime source of high-quality protein: 14-16% of the animal protein consumed world-wide; over one billion people rely on fish as their primary source of animal protein. Fish is among the most common food allergens.

There are over 27,000 species of fish, making them the most diverse group of vertebrates. However, only a small number of the total species are considered food fish and are commonly eaten.

Some common food fish species are listed below:

- Anchovy
- Carp
- Catfish
- Chilean sea bass
- Cod
- Eel
- Haddock
- Herring
- Mackerel

- Salmon
- Sardine
- Scad
- Snapper
- Tilapia
- Trout
- Tuna

Perishability

Fish is a highly perishable product. The *fishy* smell of dead fish is due to the breakdown of amino acids into biogenic amines and ammonia.

Live food fish are sometimes transported in tanks at high expense for an international market that prefers its seafood killed immediately before it is cooked. Delivery of live fish without water is also being explored. While some seafood restaurants keep live fish in aquaria for display purposes or for cultural beliefs, the majority of live fish are kept for dining customers. The live food fish trade in Hong Kong, for example, is estimated to have driven imports of live food fish to more than 15,000 tonnes in 2000. Worldwide sales that year were estimated at US$400 million, according to the World Resources Institute.

Preservation

Fresh fish is a highly perishable food product, so it must be eaten promptly or discarded; it can be kept for only a short time. In many countries, fresh fish are filleted and displayed for sale on a bed of crushed ice or refrigerated. Fresh fish is most commonly found near bodies of water, but the advent of refrigerated train and truck transportation has made fresh fish more widely available inland.

Long term preservation of fish is accomplished in a variety of ways. The oldest and still most widely used techniques are drying and salting. Desiccation (complete drying) is commonly used to preserve fish such as cod. Partial drying and salting is popular for the preservation of fish like herring and mackerel. Fish such as salmon, tuna, and herring are cooked and canned. Most fish are filleted prior to canning, but some small fish (e.g. sardines) are only decapitated and gutted prior to canning.

Fish can be prepared in a variety of ways. It can be uncooked (raw) (*cf.* sashimi). It can be cured by marinating (*cf.* escabeche), pickling (*cf.* pickled herring), or smoking (*cf.* smoked salmon). Or it can be cooked by baking, frying (*cf.* fish and chips), grilling, poaching (*cf.* court-bouillon), or steaming. Many of the preservation techniques used in different cultures have since become unnecessary but are still performed for their resulting taste and texture when consumed.

Fish, especially saltwater fish, is high in Omega 3 fatty acids, which are heart-friendly, and a regular diet of fish is highly recommended by nutritionists. This is supposed to be one of the major causes of reduced risk for cardiovascular diseases in Eskimos. It has been suggested that the longer lifespan of Japanese and Nordic populations may be partially due to their higher consumption of fish and seafood. The Mediterranean diet is likewise based on a rich intake of fish.

Fish products have been shown to contain varying amounts of heavy metals, particularly mercury and fat-soluble pollutants from water pollution. According to the US Food and Drug Administration (FDA), the risk from mercury by eating fish and shellfish is not a health concern for most people. However, certain seafood contains sufficient mercury to harm an unborn baby or young child's developing nervous system. The FDA makes three recommendations for child-bearing women and young children:

- Do not eat Shark, Swordfish, King Mackerel, or Tilefish because they contain high levels of mercury.
- Eat up to 12 ounces (2 average meals) a week of a variety of fish and shellfish that are lower in mercury. Five of the most commonly eaten fish that are low in mercury are shrimp, canned light tuna, salmon, pollock, and catfish. Another commonly eaten fish, albacore ("white") tuna has more

mercury than canned light tuna. So, when choosing your two meals of fish and shellfish, you may eat up to 6 ounces (one average meal) of albacore tuna per week.

- Check local advisories about the safety of fish caught by family and friends in your local lakes, rivers, and coastal areas. If no advice is available, eat up to 6 ounces (one average meal) per week of fish you catch from local waters, but don't consume any other fish during that week.

These recommendations are also advised when feeding fish and shellfish to young children, but in smaller portions.

Parasites in fish are a natural occurrence and common. Though not a health concern in thoroughly cooked fish, parasites are a concern when consumers eat raw or lightly preserved fish such as sashimi, sushi, ceviche, and gravlax. The popularity of the such raw fish dishes makes it important for consumers to be aware of this risk. Raw fish should be frozen to an internal temperature of -20°C (-4°F) for at least 7 days to kill parasites. It is important to be aware that home freezers may not be cold enough to kill parasites.

Traditionally, fish that live some or part of their lives in fresh water were considered unsuitable for sashimi due to the possibility of parasites (see Sashimi article). Parasitic infections from freshwater fish are a serious problem in some parts of the world, particularly Southeast Asia. Fish that spend part of their life cycle in brackish or freshwater, like salmon are a particular problem. A study in Seattle, Washington showed that 100% of wild salmon had roundworm larvae capable of infecting people. In the same study farm raised salmon did not have any roundworm larvae.

Fish are the most common food to obstruct the airway and cause choking which was responsible for about 4,500 accidents a year in the UK as of 1998.

Fish as Meat

The term "meat" has animal, vegetable and fungal applications - to wit, the "meat" of a tomato (distinct from the juice and seeds), the "meat" of a mushroom cap (as distinct from spores, gills and stems); and the edible flesh of any animal, as well as its edible organs(both as distinct from the bones, skin, feathers, fur, scales, etc.), are called "meat".

As a generic culinary and butchery term, "meat" refers to the muscular flesh of a mammal. This is the definition most commonly applied by governments in meat product regulation and food labeling, and in religious rites and rituals. Edible birds and fish/seafood are not "meat" under this application but are treated separately from mammals. Likewise, amphibians and reptiles, not to mention the "meat" of edible insects, arachnids, and so on.

Religious rites and rituals regarding food also tend to apply this distinction, classifying the birds of the air and the fish of the sea separately from land-bound mammals. Sea-bound mammals are often treated as fish under religious laws - as in Jewish dietary law, which forbids the eating of whale, dolphin, porpoise, and orca because they are not "fish with fins and scales"; nor, as mammals, do they "cheweth the cud and divideth the hoof."

Otherwise, seasonal religious prohibitions against eating meat do not usually include fish. For example, meat was forbidden during Lent and on all Fridays of the year in pre-Vatican II Roman Catholicism, but fish was permitted (as were eggs). (See Fasting in Catholicism.) In Eastern Orthodoxy, fish is permitted on some fast days when meat is forbidden, but stricter fast days also prohibit fish with fins and scales, while permitting invertebrate seafood such as shrimp and oysters, considering them "fish without blood."

Muslim (*halaal*) and Jewish (*kosher*) practice treat fish differently from other animal foods. Some Buddhists and Hindus (Brahmins of West Bengal State in India) abjure meat, but not fish. From a Buddhist point of view, if a person abjures meat, he or she is most likely to abjure fish as well. Fish is also meat since it comes from animal.

Pescetarians, for example, may consume fish based solely upon the fact that the fish are not factory farmed as land animals are (i.e., their problem is with the capitalist-industrial production of meat, not with the consumption of animal foods themselves). Some eat fish with the justification that fish have less sophisticated nervous systems than land-dwelling animals. Others may choose to consume only wild fish based upon the lack of confinement, while choosing to not consume fish that have been farmed.

Sustainable Seafood

Sustainable seafood is seafood from either fished or farmed sources that can maintain or increase production in the future without jeopardizing the ecosystems from which it was acquired. The sustainable seafood movement has gained momentum as more people become aware about both overfishing and environmentally-destructive fishing methods.

In general, slow-growing fish that reproduce late in life, such as orange roughy, are quite vulnerable to overfishing. Seafood species that grow quickly and breed young, such as anchovies and sardines, are much more resistant to overfishing. Several organizations, including the Marine Stewardship Council, and Friend of the Sea, certify seafood fisheries as sustainable.

Marine Stewardship Council

The Marine Stewardship Council (MSC) is an international non-profit organization that runs a certification and eco-labelling programme for sustainable seafood.

The MSC was founded in 1997 as a unique green-business partnership between WWF, the global environmental conservation organization, and Unilever, at the time a major seafood processor. It has been fully independent since 1999.

Fisheries that meet the MSC standard for a sustainable fishery can use the blue MSC ecolabel (shown right) on their seafood products. This enables consumers to easily identify sustainable seafood when shopping or dining out. The MSC website lists outlets selling MSC-certified seafood.

As of July 2008, there are over 1,600 MSC-labelled seafood products sold in 36 countries around the world Approximately

7% of the world's edible wild seafood catch comes from fisheries engaged in the MSC program. 30 fisheries have been independently certified as meeting the MSC's environmental standard for sustainable fishing and over 70 are currently undergoing assessment. Another 20 to 30 are in confidential pre-assessment. Together the fisheries record annual catches of over 4 million tonnes of seafood. They represent 42 percent of the world's wild salmon catch, 40 percent of the world's prime whitefish catch, and 18 percent of the world's lobster catches for human consumption.

The MSC standard for a sustainable fishery looks at 3 aspects of a fishery:

1. The condition of the fish stock(s) of the fishery - this examines if there are enough fish to ensure that the fishery is sustainable.

2. The impact of the fishery on the marine ecosystem - this examines the effect that fishing has on the immediate marine environment including other fish species, marine mammals and seabirds.

3. The fishery management system - this evaluates the rules and procedures that are in place to maintain a sustainable fishery and to ensure that the impact on the marine environment is minimised.

The MSC has the only seafood ecolabel that is consistent with the ISEAL Code of Good Practice for Setting Social and Environmental Standards and UN FAO guidelines for fisheries certification. The FAO 'Guidelines for the Eco-labelling of Fish and Fishery Products from Marine Capture Fisheries', require that credible fishery certification and ecolabelling schemes include:

- Objective, third-party fishery assessment utilising scientific evidence;
- Transparent processes with built-in stakeholder consultation and objection procedures;
- Standards based on the sustainability of target species, ecosystems and management practices.

The MSC has succeeded in bringing together a broad coalition of supporters from several organizations and businesses around the world with a stake in the future of seafood. The MSC works through a multi-stakeholder partnership approach, taking into account the views of all those seeking to secure a sustainable future.

Friend of the Sea

Friend of the Sea is a project for the certification and promotion of seafood from sustainable fisheries and sustainable aquaculture. It is the only certification scheme which, with the same logo, certifies both wild-caught and farmed seafood. Friend of the Sea started as a project of the Earth Island Institute, the NGO which operates the successful International Dolphin-Safe project (www.dolphinsafetuna.org). It is participated by some of the main retailers world wide, such as Carrefour Italy, Coop Italia, Eroski, Manor and Finiper. Some important producers have also undergone their products to assessment for certification.

Friend of the Sea's criteria compliance is verified by independent accredited certification bodies. Essential criteria for fisheries are the following (all criteria are described in documents downloadable from website): (a) the product should not originate from overexploited (nor depleted, data deficient or recovering) stocks; (b) fishing method should not impact the seabed; (c) fishing method should be selective (maximum 8% discard – average WW according to FAO 2005); (d) fishery should respect all legal requirements. A list of Friend of the Sea conforming origins and approved fishing methods is available under the 'Sustainable Fisheries' menu on the web site.

Seafood Watch

The Monterey Bay Aquarium's Seafood Watch Program, although not an official certifying body like the MSC, also provides guidance on the sustainability of certain fish species. Seafood Watch takes into account the:

1. Inherent vulnerability of the species to fishing pressure

2. Status of the species population.
3. Nature and extent of bycatch.
4. Effect of fishing practices on habitats and ecosystems.
5. Effectiveness of the fishery management.

Overfishing

Overfishing occurs when fishing activities reduce fish stocks below an acceptable level. This can occur in any body of water from a pond to the oceans.

Ultimately overfishing may lead to resource depletion in cases of subsidised fishing, low biological growth rates and critical low biomass levels (e.g. by critical depensation growth properties). Particularly, overfishing of sharks has led to the upset of entire marine ecosystems.

The ability of the fisheries to naturally recover also depends on whether the conditions of the ecosystems are suitable for population growth. Dramatic changes in species composition may establish other equilibrium energy flows that involve other species compositions than had been present before (ecosystem shift). (For example: remove nearly all the trout, the carp take over and make it near impossible for the trout to re-establish a breeding population.)

A major international scientific study released in November 2008 in the journal *Science* found that about one-third of all fishing stocks worldwide have collapsed (with a collapse being defined as a decline to less than 10% of their maximum observed abundance), and that if current trends continue all fish stocks worldwide will collapse within fifty years.

The FAO State of World Fisheries and Aquaculture 2008 report estimates that in 2008 of the main fish stocks or groups of resources for which assessment information is available, "approximately one-quarter were overexploited, depleted or recovering from depletion (16%, 7% and 1% respectively) and needed rebuilding."

The threat of overfishing is not limited to the target species only. As commercial trawlers resort to deeper and deeper waters to fill their nets, they have begun to threaten delicate deep-sea ecosystems and the fish that inhabit them, such as the coelacanth. It is estimated that 10% of large predatory fish remain compared to levels before commercial fishing. Many fisheries experts, however, consider this claim to be exaggerated with respect to tuna populations.

From 1950 (18 million tonnes) to 1969 (56 million tonnes) fishfood production grew by about 5% each year; from 1969 onward production has raised 8% annually. It is expected that this demand will continue to rise, and Mari Culture Systems estimated in 2002 that, by 2010, seafood production would have to increase by over 15.5 million tonnes to meet the desire of Earth's growing population. This is likely to further aggravate the problem of overfishing, unless aquaculture technology expands to meet the needs of human population.

Overfishing has depleted fish populations to the point that large scale commercial fishing, on average around the world, is not economically viable without government assistance. By the 1980s, economists estimated that for every $1 earned fishing, $1.77 had to be spent in catching and marketing the fish. Some species' stocks are so depleted that less desirable species are labeled and marketed under the names of more expensive ones ("species substitutions"). For example, genetic analysis shows that approximately 70% of fish sold as the highly-prized "red snapper" (*Lutjanus campechanus*) are other species.

Instances of overfishing

Examples of the outcomes from overfishing exist in areas such as the North Sea of Europe and the Grand Banks of North America. In these locations, overfishing has not only proved disastrous to fish stocks but also to the fishing communities relying on the harvest. Like other extractive industries such as forestry and hunting, fishery is susceptible to economic interaction between ownership or stewardship and sustainability, otherwise known as the tragedy of the commons.

The Peruvian coastal anchovy fisheries crashed in the 1970s after overfishing, following an El Niño season which largely depleted anchovies from its waters. Anchovies had previously been a major natural resource in Peru; indeed, 1971 alone yielded 10.2 million metric tons of anchovies. However, in the following year, and the four after that, the Peruvian fleet's catch amounted to only about 4 million tons This was a major loss to Peru's economy.

The collapse of the cod fishery off Newfoundland, and the 1992 decision by Canada to impose an indefinite moratorium on the Grand Banks, is a dramatic example of the consequences of overfishing.

The sole fisheries in the Irish Sea, the west English Channel, and other locations have become overfished to the point of virtual collapse, according to the UK government's official Biodiversity Action Plan. The United Kingdom has created elements within this plan to attempt to restore this fishery, but the expanding global human population and the expanding demand for fish has reached a point where demand for food threatens the stability of these fisheries, if not the species' survival.

Acceptable Levels

The notion of overfishing hinges on what is meant by an *acceptable level* of fishing. More precise biological and bioeconomic terms define acceptable level as follows:

- *Biological overfishing* occurs when fishing mortality has reached a level where the stock biomass has negative marginal growth. (Fish are being taken out of the water so quickly that the replenishment of stock by breeding slows down. If the replenishment continues to slow down for long enough, replenishment will go into reverse and the population will decrease.)
- *Economic or bioeconomic overfishing* additionally considers the cost of fishing and defines overfishing as a situation of negative marginal growth of resource rent. (Fish are being taken out of the water so quickly that the growth in the profitability of fishing slows down. If this continues for long enough, profitability will decrease.)
- A more dynamic definition of *economic overfishing* may also include a relevant discount rate and present value of flow of resource rent over all future catches.

The Traffic Light colour convention, showing the concept of Harvest Control Rule (HCR), specifying when a rebuilding plan is mandatory in terms of precautionary and limit reference points for spawning biomass and fishing mortality rate.

Harvest Control Rule

A current model for predicting acceptable levels is the Harvest Control Rule (HCR). The HCR is a variable over which management has some direct control as a function of some indicator of stock status. Constant catch and constant fishing mortality are two types of simple harvest control rules.

Input-output Models

Fishing capacity can also be defined following an input or an output orientation.

- An input-oriented fishing capacity is defined as the maximum available capital stock in a fishery that is fully utilized at the maximum technical efficiency in a given time period, given resource and market conditions.
- An output-oriented fishing capacity is defined as the maximum catch a vessel (fleet) can produce if inputs are fully utilized given the biomass, the fixed inputs, the age structure of the fish stock, and the present stage of technology.

Technical efficiency of each vessel of the fleet is assumed necessary to attain this maximum catch. The degree of capacity utilization results from the comparison of the actual level of output (input) and the capacity output (input) of a vessel or a fleet.

Mitigation

With present and forecast levels of the world population it is not possible to solve the overfishing issue; however, there are mitigation measures that can save selected fisheries and forestall the collapse of others.

In order to meet the problems of overfishing, a precautionary approach and Harvest Control Rule (HCR) management principles have been introduced in the main fisheries around the world. The Traffic Light colour convention introduces sets of rules based on predefined critical values, which could be adjusted as more information is gained.

The "United Nations Convention on the Law of the Sea" treaty deals with aspects of *overfishing* in Articles 61, 62, and 65.

- Article 61 requires all coastal states to ensure that the maintenance of living resources in their exclusive economic zones is not endangered by over-exploitation. The same article addresses the maintenance or restoration of populations of species above levels at which their reproduction may become seriously threatened.
- Article 62 provides that coastal states: "shall promote the objective of optimum utilization of the living resources in the exclusive economic zone without prejudice to Article 61".
- Article 65 provides generally for the rights of, inter alia, coastal states to prohibit, limit, or regulate the exploitation of marine mammals.

Overfishing can be viewed as a case of the tragedy of the commons; in that sense, solutions would promote property rights, such as privatization and fish farming.

According to research on the British Columbia halibut fishery, where the commons has been at least partly privatized, substantial ecological and economic benefits have resulted. There is less damage to fish stocks, the fishing is safer, and fewer resources are needed to achieve a given harvest.

Another possible solution, at least for some areas, is fishing quotas, so fishermen can only legally take a certain amount of fish. A more radical possibility is declaring certain areas of the sea "no-go zones" and make fishing there strictly illegal, so the fish in that area have time to recover and repopulate.

Controlling consumer behavior and demand is a key in mitigating action. Worldwide a number of initiatives emerged to provide consumers with information regarding the conservation status of the seafood available to them. The Guide to Good Fish Guides lists a number of these.

Fishing Quotas

A model of the interaction between fish and fishers showed that when an area is closed to fishers, but there are no catch regulations such as individual transferable quotas, fish catches are temporarily increased but overall fish biomass is reduced, resulting in the opposite outcome than the one desired for fisheries. Thus, a displacement of the fleet from one locality to another will generally have little effect if the same quota is taken. As a result, management measures such as temporary closures or establishing a Marine Protected Area of fishing areas are ineffective when not combined with individual fishing quotas.

Individual Transferable Quotas

Individual transferable quotas (ITQs) are fishery rationalization instruments defined under the Magnuson-Stevens Fishery Conservation and Management Act as limited access permits to harvest quantities of fish. Fisheries scientists decide the optimal amount of fish (total allowable catch) to be harvested in a certain fishery, taking into account carrying capacity, regeneration rates and future values. Under ITQs, members of a fishery are granted rights to a percentage of the total allowable catch which can be harvested each year. These quotas can be fished, bought, sold, or leased allowing for the least cost vessels to be used. ITQs are used in New Zealand, Australia, Iceland, Canada and the United States. Only three ITQ programs have been implemented in the United States due to a moratorium supported by Ted Stevens.

In 2008 a large scale study of fisheries that used ITQ's and ones that didn't provided strong evidence that ITQ's can help to prevent collapses and restore fisheries that appear to be in decline.

Benefits of Underfishing

Deliberately underfishing in order to increase long term fish stocks has been proposed as a way fisherman can maximize their yields in the long run.

Resistance from Fishermen

The fishing capacity problem is not only related to the conservation of fish stocks but also to the sustainability of fishing activity. Causes of the fishing problem can be found in property rights regime of fishing resources. Overexploitation and rent dissipation of fishermen arise in open-access fisheries as was shown in Gordon

In open-access resources like fish stocks, the impossibility of excluding others provokes the fishermen who want to increase catch to do so effectively by taking someone else' share, intensifying competition. This provokes a capitalization process that leads them to increase their costs until they are equal to their revenue, dissipating their rent completely.

Marine Stewardship Council

The Marine Stewardship Council (MSC) is an independent, global, non-profit organization which was set up in 1997 to find a solution to the problem of overfishing. It has developed an environmental standard for sustainable and well-managed fisheries. Environmentally responsible fisheries management and practices are rewarded with the use of its blue product ecolabel. Consumers concerned about overfishing and its consequences are increasingly able to choose seafood products which have been independently assessed against the MSC's environmental standard and labeled to prove it. This enables consumers to play a part in reversing the decline of fish stocks. As of July 2008, 30 fisheries around the world have been independently assessed and certified as meeting the MSC standard, and over 70 are in assessment against the standard. There are over 1,600 seafood products sold by retailers in 36 countries around the world. Their 'where to buy' page lists all currently available certified seafood.

9

Population Dynamics of Fisheries

Introduction

A fishery is an area with an associated fish or aquatic population which is harvested for its commercial or recreational value. Fisheries can be wild or farmed. Population dynamics describes the ways in which a given population grows and shrinks over time, as controlled by birth, death, and emigration or immigration. It is the basis for understanding changing fishery patterns and issues such as habitat destruction, predation and optimal harvesting rates. The population dynamics of fisheries is used by fisheries scientists to determine sustainable yields

The basic accounting relation for population dynamics is:

$$N_1 = N_0 + B - D + I - E$$

where N_1 is the number of individuals at time 1, N_0 is the number of individuals at time 0, B is the number of individuals born, D the number that died, I the number that immigrated, and E the number that emigrated between time 0 and time 1. While immigration and emigration can be present in wild fisheries, they are usually not measured.

A fishery population is affected by three dynamic rate functions:

- *Birth rate or recruitment.* Recruitment means reaching a certain size or reproductive stage. With fisheries, recruitment usually refers to the age a fish can be caught and counted in nets.

- *Growth rate*. This measures the growth of individuals in size and length. This is important in fisheries where the population is often measured in terms of biomass.
- *Mortality*. This includes harvest mortality and natural mortality. Natural mortality includes non-human predation, disease and old age.

If these rates are measured over different time intervals, the harvestable surplus of a fishery can be determined. The harvestable surplus is the number of individuals that can be harvested from the population without affecting long term stability (average population size). The harvest within the harvestable surplus is called *compensatory mortality*, where the harvest deaths are substituting for the deaths that would otherwise occur naturally. Harvest beyond that is *additive mortality*, harvest in addition to all the animals that would have died naturally.

The first principle of population dynamics is widely regarded as the exponential law of Malthus, as modelled by the Malthusian growth model. The early period was dominated by demographic studies such as the work of Benjamin Gompertz and Pierre François Verhulst in the early 19th century, who refined and adjusted the Malthusian demographic model. A more general model formulation was proposed by F.J. Richards in 1959, by which the models of Gompertz, Verhulst and also Ludwig von Bertalanffy are covered as special cases of the general formulation.

Population Size

The population size (usually denoted by N) is the number of individual organisms in a population.

The effective population size (N_e) was defined by Sewall Wright, who wrote two landmark papers on it. He defined it as "the number of breeding individuals in an idealized population that would show the same amount of dispersion of allele frequencies under random genetic drift or the same amount of inbreeding as the population under consideration". It is a basic parameter in many models in population genetics. *Ne* is usually less than *N* (the absolute population size).

Small population size results in increased genetic drift. Population bottlenecks are when population size reduces for a short period of time.

Overpopulation may indicate any case in which the population of any species of animal may exceed the carrying capacity of its ecological niche.

Virtual population analysis (VPA) is a modelling technique commonly used in fisheries science for reconstructing historical fish numbers using information on death of individuals each year. This death is usually partitioned into catch by fisheries and natural mortality.

The VPA is the most commonly used term to refer to cohort reconstruction techniques used in fisheries. It is virtual in the sense that the population size is not observed or measured directly but is inferred or back-calculated to have been a certain size in the past in order to support the observed fish catches and an assumed death rate owing to non-fishery related causes.

The minimum viable population (MVP) is a lower bound on the population of a species, such that it can survive in the wild. More specifically MVP is the smallest possible size at which a biological population can exist without facing extinction from natural disasters or demographic, environmental, or genetic stochasticity. The term "population" refers to the population of a species in the wild.

As a reference standard, MVP is usually given with a population survival probability of somewhere between ninety and ninety-five percent and calculated for between one hundred and one thousand years into the future.

The MVP can be calculated using computer simulations known as population viability analyses (PVA), where populations are modelled and future population dynamics are projected.

Maximum Sustainable Yield

In population ecology and economics, maximum sustainable yield or MSY is, theoretically, the largest catch that can be taken from a fishery stock over an indefinite period. Under the assumption of logistic growth, the MSY will be exactly at half the carrying capacity of a species, as this is the stage at when population growth is highest. The maximum sustainable yield is usually higher than the optimum sustainable yield.

This logistic model of growth is produced by a population introduced to a new habitat or with very poor numbers going through a lag phase of slow growth at first. Once it reaches a foothold population it will go through a rapid growth rate that will start to level off once the species approaches carrying capacity. The idea of maximum sustained yield is to decrease population density to the point of highest growth rate possible. This changes the number of the population, but the new number can be maintained indefinitely, ideally.

The MSY is extensively used for fisheries management. Unlike the logistic (Schaefer) model, MSY in most modern fisheries models occurs at around 30% of the unexploited population size. This fraction differs among populations depending on the life history of the species and the age-specific selectivity of the fishing method.

Overfishing

The Traffic Light colour convention, showing the concept of Harvest Control Rule (HCR), specifying when a rebuilding plan is mandatory in terms of precautionary and limit reference points for spawning biomass and fishing mortality rate.

A current operational model used by some fisheries for predicting acceptable levels is the Harvest Control Rule (HCR). This formalizes and summarizes a management strategy which can actively adapt to subsequent feedback. The HCR is a variable over which the management has some direct control and describes how the harvest is intended to be controlled by management in relation to the state of some indicator of stock status. For example, a harvest control rule can describe the various values of fishing mortality which will be aimed at for various values of the stock abundance. Constant catch and constant fishing mortality are two types of simple harvest control rules.

- *Biological overfishing* occurs when fishing mortality has reached a level where the stock biomass has negative marginal growth (slowing down biomass growth), as indicated by the red area in the figure. Fish are being taken out of the water so quickly that the replenishment of stock by breeding slows down. If the replenishment continues to slow down for long enough, replenishment will go into reverse and the population will decrease.
- *Economic or bioeconomic overfishing* additionally considers the cost of fishing and defines overfishing as a situation of negative marginal growth of resource rent. Fish are being taken out of the water so quickly that the growth in the profitability of fishing slows down. If this continues for long enough, profitability will decrease.

A metapopulation is a group of spatially separated populations of the same species which interact at some level. The term was coined by Richard Levins in 1969. The idea has been most broadly applied to species in naturally or artificially fragmented habitats. In Levins' own words, it consists of "a population of populations".

A metapopulation generally consists of several distinct populations together with areas of suitable habitat which are currently unoccupied. Each population cycles in relative independence of the other populations and eventually goes extinct as a consequence of demographic stochasticity (fluctuations in population size due to random demographic events); the smaller the population, the more prone it is to extinction.

Although individual populations have finite life-spans, the population as a whole is often stable because immigrants from one population (which may, for example, be experiencing a population boom) are likely to re-colonize habitat which has been left open by the extinction of another population. They may also emigrate to a small population and rescue that population from extinction (called the *rescue effect*).

Age Class Structure

Age can be determined by counting growth rings in fish scales, otoliths, cross-sections of fin spines for species with thick spines such as triggerfish, or teeth for a few species. Each method has its merits and drawbacks. Fish scales are easiest to obtain, but may be unreliable if scales have fallen off of the fish and new ones grown in their places. Fin spines may be unreliable for the same reason, and most fish do not have spines of sufficient thickness for clear rings to be visible. Otoliths will have stayed with the fish throughout its life history, but obtaining them requires killing the fish. Also, otoliths often require more preparation before ageing can occur.

An age class structure with gaps in it, for instance a regular bell curve for the population of 1-5-year old fish, excepting a very low population for the 3-year old, implies a bad spawning year 3 year ago in that species.

Often fish in younger age class structures have very low numbers because they were small enough to slip through the sampling nets, and may in fact have a very healthy population.

A population cycle occurs where populations rise and fall over a predictable period of time. There are some species where population numbers have reasonably predictable patterns of change although the full reasons for population cycles is one of the major unsolved ecological problems. There are a number of factors which influence population change such as availability of food, predators, diseases and climate.

Trophic Cascades

Trophic cascades occur when predators in a food chain suppress the abundance of their prey, thereby releasing the next lower trophic level from predation (or herbivory if the intermediate trophic level is an herbivore). For example, if the abundance of large piscivorous fish is increased in a lake, the abundance of their prey, zooplanktivorous fish, should decrease, large zooplankton abundance should increase, and phytoplankton biomass should decrease. This theory has stimulated new research in many areas of ecology. Trophic cascades may also be important for understanding the effects of removing top predators from food webs, as humans have done in many places through hunting and fishing activities.

Classic Examples

In lakes, piscivorous fish can dramatically reduce populations of zooplanktivorous fish, zooplanktivorous fish can dramatically alter freshwater zooplankton communities, and zooplankton grazing can in turn have large impacts on phytoplankton communities. Removal of piscivorous fish can change lake water from clear to green by allowing phytoplankton to flourish.

In the Eel River, in Northern California, fish (steelhead and roach) consume fish larvae and predatory insects. These smaller predators prey on midge larvae, which feed on algae. Removal of the larger fish increases the abundance of algae.

In Pacific kelp forests, sea otters feed on sea urchins. In areas where sea otters have been hunted to extinction, sea urchins increase in abundance and decimate kelp.

A recent theory, the mesopredator release hypothesis, states that the decline of top predators in an ecosystem results in increased populations of medium-sized predators (mesopredators).

Predator-prey Equations

The classic predator-prey equations are a pair of first order, non-linear, differential equations used to describe the dynamics of biological systems in which two species interact, one a predator and one its prey. They were proposed independently by Alfred J. Lotka in 1925 and Vito Volterra in 1926.

An extension to these are the competitive Lotka-Volterra equations, which provide a simple model of the population dynamics of species competing for some common resource.

In the 1930s Alexander Nicholson and Victor Bailey developed a model to describe the population dynamics of a coupled predator-prey system. The model assumes that predators search for prey at random, and that both predators and prey are assumed to be distributed in a non-contagious ("clumped") fashion in the environment.

Environmental Effects of Fishing

The environmental effects of fishing can be divided into issues that involve the availability of fish to be caught, such as overfishing, sustainable fisheries, and fisheries management; and issues that involve the impact of fishing on the environment, such as by-catch.

These conservation issues are part of marine conservation, and are addressed in fisheries science programs. There is a growing gap between how many fish are available to be caught and humanity's desire to catch them, a problem that gets worse as the world population grows.

Similar to other environmental issues, there can be conflict between the fishermen who depend on fishing for their livelihoods and fishery scientists who realise that if future fish populations are to be sustainable then some fisheries must reduce or even close.

The journal *Science* published a four-year study in November 2006, which predicted that, at prevailing trends, the world would run out of wild-caught seafood in 2048. The scientists stated that the decline was a result of overfishing, pollution and other environmental factors that were reducing the population of fisheries at the same time as their ecosystems were being degraded. Yet again the analysis has met criticism as being fundamentally flawed, and many fishery management officials, industry representatives and scientists challenge the findings, although the debate continues. Many countries, such as Tonga, the United States, Australia and New Zealand, and international management bodies have taken steps to appropriately manage marine resources.

Effects on Habitat

Some fishing techniques also may cause habitat destruction. Dynamite fishing and cyanide fishing, which are illegal in many places, harm surrounding habitat. Bottom trawling, the practice of pulling a fishing net along the sea bottom behind trawlers, removes around 5 to 25% of an area's seabed life on a single run. A 2005 report of the UN Millennium Project, commissioned by UN Secretary-General Kofi Annan, recommended the elimination of bottom trawling on the high seas by 2006 to protect seamounts and other ecologically sensitive habitats.

Overfishing has also been widely reported due to increases in the volume of fishing hauls to feed a quickly growing number of consumers. This has led to the breakdown of some sea ecosystems and several fishing industries whose catch has been greatly diminished The extinction of many species has also been reported. According to an FAO estimate, over 70% of the world's fish species are either fully exploited or depleted. According to Nitin Desai, Secretary General of the 2002 World Summit on Sustainable Development, "Overfishing cannot continue, the depletion of fisheries poses a major threat to the food supply of millions of people."

The cover story of the May 15, 2003 issue of the science journal *Nature* - with Dr. Ransom A. Myers, an internationally prominent fisheries biologist (Dalhousie University, Halifax, Canada) as the lead author - was devoted to a summary of the scientific information. The story asserted that, as compared with 1950 levels, only a remnant (in some instances, as little as 10%) of all large ocean-fish stocks are left in the seas. These large ocean fish are the species at the top of the food chains (e.g., tuna, cod, among others). However, this article was subsequently criticized as being fundamentally flawed, although much debate still exists and the majority of fisheries scientists now consider the results irrelevant with respect to large pelagics (the open seas).

Fishing may disrupt food webs by targeting specific, in-demand species. There might be too much fishing of prey species such as sardines and anchovies, thus reducing the food supply for the predators. It may also cause the increase of prey species when the target fishes are predator species such as salmon and tuna. Fisheries can reduce fish stocks that cetaceans rely on for food.

By-catch

By-catch is the portion of the catch that is not the target species. These are either kept to be sold or discarded. In some instances the discarded portion is known as discards. Many governments have implemented fisheries management policies designed to curb the environmental impact of fishing. Fishing conservation aims to control the human activities that may completely decrease a fish stock or washout an entire aquatic environment. These laws include the quotas on the total catch of particular species in a fishery, limits on the number of vessels allowed in specific areas, and the imposition of seasonal restrictions on fishing.

In 2008 a large scale study of fisheries that used individual transferable quotas and ones that didn't provided strong evidence that individual transferable quotas can help to prevent collapses and restore fisheries that appear to be in decline. Fish farming has been proposed as a more sustainable alternative to traditional capture of wild fish. However, fish farming has been found to have negative impacts on nearby wild fish. The environmental impact of recreational fishing may be alleviated to some extent by catch and release fishing

Jellyfish

Jellyfish are free-swimming members of the phylum Cnidaria. They have several different basic morphologies that represent several different cnidarian classes including the Scyphozoa (about 200 species), Staurozoa (about 50 species), Cubozoa (about 20 species), and Hydrozoa (about 1000-1500 species that make jellyfish and many more that do not) . The jellyfish in these groups are also called, respectively, scyphomedusae, stauromedusae, cubomedusae, and hydromedusae; "medusa" (plural "medusae") is another word for jellyfish. Jellyfish are found in every ocean, from the surface to the deep sea. Some hydrozoan jellyfish, or hydromedusae, are also found in fresh water. Most of the information about jellyfish that follows in this article is about scyphozoan jellyfish, or scyphomedusae. These are the big, often colorful, jellyfish that are common in coastal zones worldwide.

In its broadest sense, the term jellyfish is sometimes used also to refer to members of the phylum Ctenophora. Although not closely related to cnidarian jellyfish, ctenophores are also free-swimming planktonic carnivores, are also generally transparent or translucent, and occur in shallow to deep portions of all the world's oceans. Ctenophores move using eight rows of fused cilia that beat in metachronal waves that diffract light, so that they sparkle with all of the colors of the rainbow. The rest of this article deals only with jellyfish in the phylum Cnidaria.

Body Systems

A jellyfish detects the touch of other animals using a nervous system called a "nerve net", located in its epidermis. Touch stimuli are conducted by nerve rings, through the rhopalial lappet, located around the animal's body, to the nerve cells. Some jellyfish also have ocelli: light-sensitive organs that do not form images but are used to determine up from down, responding to sunlight shining on the water's surface. They also sting when another organism touches their tentacles.

Jellyfish don't have specialized digestive, osmoregulatory, central nervous, respiratory, or circulatory systems. They digest using the gastrodermal lining of the gastrovascular cavity, where nutrients are absorbed. They do not need a respiratory system since their skin is thin enough that the body is oxygenated by diffusion. They have limited control over movement and mostly free-float, but can use the hydrostatic skeleton of the water pouch to accomplish vertical movement through pulsations of the disc-like body.

Jellyfish Blooms

Jellyfish are, by the nature of their life cycles, "bloomy". Their presence in the ocean is usually seasonal, responding to the availability of prey, which is seasonal in most places, increasing with temperature and sunshine in the spring and summer. Ocean currents tend to congregate jellyfish into large swarms or "blooms", consisting of hundreds or thousands of individuals. In addition to sometimes being concentrated by ocean currents, blooms can furthermore be the result of unusually high populations in some years. The formation of these blooms is a complex process that depends on ocean currents, nutrients, temperature and ambient oxygen concentrations. The news media recently has been full of stories about increases in jellyfish blooms . It is important to realize, however, that there is very little data about changes in global jellyfish populations over time, besides "impressions" in the public memory. In most places in the world, scientists have no quantitative data about what jellyfish populations used to be like, or in fact, quantitative data about what is happening in the present[8]. Recent speculations about increases in jellyfish populations often are based on no "before" data.

According to Claudia Mills of the University of Washington, increasing frequency of jellyfish blooms globally might be attributed to humans' impact on marine systems. She says that in some locations jellyfish may be filling ecological niches formerly occupied by overfished creatures, but notes that we lack data to show that is indeed true ellyfish researcher Marsh Youngbluth further clarifies that "jellyfish feed on the same kinds of prey as adult and young fish, so if fish are removed from the equation, jellyfish are likely to move in."

Some jellyfish populations that have shown clear increases in the past few decades are "invasive" species, newly arrived from other parts of the world: examples of regions with troublesome non-native jellyfish include the Black Sea and the Caspian Sea, the Baltic Sea, the eastern Mediterranean coasts of Egypt and Israel, and the American coast of the Gulf of Mexico. Populations of some invasive species expand rapidly because there are no natural predators in the ecosystem to check their growth - such blooms would not necessarily reflect overfishing or other environmental problems.

Aurelia sp., commonly known as the moon jellyfish, occurs in very high numbers in nearshore waters many places in the world. Several sibling species are difficult to casually distinguish.

Increased nutrients in the water, ascribed to agricultural runoff, have also been cited as an antecedent to the proliferation of jellyfish. Monty Graham, of the Dauphin Island Sea Lab in Alabama, says that "ecosystems in which there are high levels of nutrients . . . provide nourishment for the small organisms on which jellyfish feed. In waters where there is eutrophication, low oxygen levels often result, favoring jellyfish as they thrive in less oxygen-rich water than fish can tolerate. The fact that jellyfish are increasing is a symptom of something happening in the ecosystem."

By sampling sea life in a heavily fished region off the coast of Namibia, researchers found that jellyfish have overtaken fish in terms of biomass. The findings represent a careful, quantitative analysis of what has been called a "jellyfish explosion" following intense fishing in the area in the last few decades. The findings were reported by Andrew Brierley of the University of St. Andrews and his colleagues on the 11th July, 2006 issue of the journal *Current Biology* affected by jellyfish blooms include the northern Gulf of Mexico. In that case, Graham states, "Moon jellies have formed a kind of gelatinous net that stretches from Life history".

The Developmental Stages of Scyphozoan Jellyfish

Most jellyfish pass through two distinct life history phases (body forms) during their life cycle. The first is the *polypoid* stage, when the animal takes the form of a small stalk with feeding tentacles; this polyp may be sessile, living on the bottom or on similar substrata such as floats or boat-bottoms, or it may be free-floating or attached to tiny bits of free-living plankton or even (rarely) fish. Polyps generally have a mouth surrounded by tentacles that face upwards, like miniatures of the closely-related anthozoan polyps (sea anemones and corals), also of the phylum Cnidaria. Jellyfish polyps may be solitary or colonial, and some bud asexually by various means, making more polyps. Most are very small, measured in millimeters or a fraction of an inch tall.

In the second stage, the tiny polyps asexually produce jellyfish, each of which is also known as a *medusa.* Tiny jellyfish (usually only a millimeter or two across) pull away from the polyp by swimming, and then grow and feed in the plankton. Medusae have a radially symmetric, umbrella-shaped body called a *bell,* which is usually supplied with marginal tentacles - fringe-like protrusions from the border of the bell that are used to capture prey. (*Medusa* is also the word for jellyfish in Finnish, Portuguese, Romanian, Hebrew, Serbian, Croatian, Spanish, French, Italian, Hungarian, Polish, Czech, Slovak, Russian and Bulgarian.) A few species of jellyfish do not have the polyp portion of the life cycle, but go from jellyfish to the next generation of jellyfish through direct development of the fertilized eggs.

Jellyfish are dioecious; that is, they are either male or female. In most cases, to reproduce, both males and females release sperm or eggs into the surrounding water, where the (unprotected) eggs are fertilized and mature into new organisms. In a few species, the sperm swim into the mouth of the female, allowing the fertilization of the ova within the female's body. Moon jellies use a different process, in which the eggs become lodged in pits on the oral arms, which form a temporary brood chamber to accommodate fertilization and early development.

After fertilization and initial growth, a larval form, called the planula, develops from the egg. The planula is a small larva covered with cilia. It settles onto a firm surface and develops into a polyp. The polyp is cup-shaped with tentacles surrounding a single orifice, resembling a tiny sea anemone. After an interval of growth, the polyp begins reproducing sexually by budding and, in the Scyphozoa, is called a *segmenting polyp,* or a scyphistoma. New scyphistomae may be produced by budding or new, immature jellys called ephyrae may be formed. A few jellyfish species are also capable of producing new medusae by budding directly from the medusan stage; such budding has been described from the tentacle bulbs, the manubrium (above the mouth), or the gonads of hydromedusae (each species bud only from one location). Fission of medksae (splitting in half) has been described for a few of species of hydromedusae.

Some of the most common and important jellyfish predators are other species of jellyfish, some of which are specialists in eating jellies. Other predators of jellyfish include tuna, shark, swordfish, and at least one species of Pacific salmon, as well as sea turtles. Sea birds sometimes pick symbiotic crustaceans from the bells of jellyfish near the surface of the sea, inevitably feeding also on the jellyfish hosts of these amphipods or young crabs and shrimp.

Jellyfish lifespans typically range from a few hours (in the case of some very small hydromedusae) to several months. The life span and maximum size of each species is unique. One unusual species is reported to live as long as 30 years and another species, *Turritopsis dohrnii as T. nutricula,* is said to be effectively immortal because of its ability to transform between medusa and polyp, thereby escaping death[12]. Most of the large coastal jellyfish live about 2 to 6 months, during which they grow from a millimeter or two to many centimeters in diameter. They feed continuously and grow to adult size fairly rapidly. After reaching adult size (which varies by species), jellyfish spawn daily if there is enough food in the ecosystem. In most jellyfish species, spawning is controlled by light, so the entire population spawns at about the same time of day, often at either dusk or dawn.

Etymology and Taxonomic History of Jellyfish

Since jellyfish are not fish, some people consider the term "jellyfish" a misnomer, and American public aquaria have popularized use of the terms "jellies" or "sea jellies" instead. Others find the word "jellyfish" to be equally useful and picturesque. The word "jellyfish" is used to denote several different kinds of cnidarians including scyphozoans, staurozoans (stalked jellyfish), hydrozoans, and cubozoans (box jellyfish). In its broadest usage, some people also include members of the phylum Ctenophora when they are referring to jellyfish.

Scyphozoan Jellyfish

The class name, *Scyphozoa,* comes from the Greek word *skyphos,* denoting a kind of drinking cup and alluding to the cup shape of the organism. A group of jellyfish is sometimes fancifully called a "smack".

Importance to Humans

Jellyfish are an important source of food to the Chinese community and in many Asian countries. Only scyphozoan jellyfish belonging to the order Rhizostomeae are harvested for food; about 12 of the approximately 85 known species of Rhizostomeae are being harvested and sold on international markets. Most of the harvest takes place in southeast Asia Rhizostomes, especially *Rhopilema esculentum* in China and *Stomolophus meleagris* (cannonball jellyfish) in the United States, are favoured because they are typically larger and have more rigid bodies than other scyphozoans. Furthermore, their toxins are innocuous to humans.

Traditional processing methods, carried out by a Jellyfish Master, involve a 20 to 40 day multi-phase procedure in which the umbrella and oral arms are treated with a mixture of table salt and alum, and compressed. The gonads and mucous membranes are removed prior to salting. Processing reduces liquidation, off-odors and the growth of spoilage organisms, and makes the jellyfish drier and more acidic, producing a "crunchy and crispy texture." Jellyfish prepared this way retain 7-10% of their original, raw weight, and the processed product contains approximately 95% water and 4-5% protein, making it a relatively low calorie food. Freshly processed jellyfish has a white, creamy color and turns yellow or brown during prolonged storage.

In China, processed jellyfish are desalted by soaking in water overnight and eaten cooked or raw. The dish is often served shredded with a dressing of oil, soy sauce, vinegar and sugar, or as a salad with vegetables. In Japan, cured jellyfish are rinsed, cut into strips and served with vinegar as an appetizer. Desalted, ready-to-eat products are also available.

Fisheries have begun harvesting cannonball jellyfish along the southern Atlantic coast of the United States and in the Gulf of Mexico for export to Asian nations.

In Biotechnology

In 1961, green fluorescent protein (GFP) was discovered in the jellyfish *Aequorea victoria* by scientists studying bioluminescence. This protein has since become a quite useful tool in biology. Its use is mainly for scientists studying in which tissues genes are expressed. The technique, using genetic engineering, fuses the gene of interest to the gene of GFP. The fused DNA is then put into a cell, to generate either a cell line or (via IVF techniques) an entire animal bearing the gene. In the cell or animal, the artificial gene gets turned on in the same tissues and the same time as the normal gene. But instead of making the normal protein, the gene makes GFP. One can then find out what tissues express that protein – or at what stage of development – by shining light on the animal or cell, and looking for the green fluorescence. The fluorescence shows where the gene of interest is expressed. Jellyfish are also harvested for their collagen, which can be used for a variety of scientific applications including the treatment of rheumatoid arthritis.

Jellyfish are commonly displayed in aquaria in many countries. Often the tank's background is blue and the animals are illuminated by side light to produce a high contrast effect. In natural conditions, many jellies are so transparent that they are almost impossible to see.

Holding jellyfish in captivity presents other problems. For one, they are not adapted to closed spaces. They depend on currents to transport them from place to place. To compensate for this, professional exhibits feature precise water flows, typically in circular tanks to prevent specimens from becoming trapped in corners. The Monterey Bay Aquarium uses a modified version of the *kreisel* (German for "spinning top") for this purpose.

Toxicity to Humans

The Lion's mane jellyfish, *Cyanea capillata,* is known for its painful, but rarely fatal, sting.

When stung by a jellyfish, first aid may be needed immediately. The stings of Scyphozoan jellyfish are not generally deadly, though some species of the completely separate class Cubozoa (box jellyfish), such as the famous and especially toxic Irukandji, can be fatal. However, even nonfatal jellyfish stings are known to be extremely painful. Serious stings may cause anaphylaxis and may result in death. Hence, people stung by jellyfish must get out of the water to avoid drowning. In serious cases, advanced professional care must be sought. This care may include administration of an antivenin and other supportive care such as required to treat the symptoms of anaphylactic shock.

There are three goals of first aid for uncomplicated jellyfish stings: prevent injury to rescuers, inactivate the nematocysts, and remove any tentacles stuck on the patient. To prevent injury to rescuers, barrier clothing should be worn. This protection may include anything from panty hose to wet suits to full-body sting-proof suits. Inactivating the nematocysts, or stinging cells, prevents further injection of venom into the patient.

The sting of some species of *Mastigias* have no discernible effect on humans.

Vinegar (3 to 10% aqueous acetic acid) should be applied for box jellyfish stings. inegar, however, is not recommended for Portuguese Man o' War stings. In the case of stings on or around the eyes, vinegar may be placed on a towel and dabbed around the eyes, but not in them. Salt water may also be used in case vinegar is not readily available Fresh water should not be used if the sting occurred in salt water, as a change in tonicity can cause the release of additional venom. Rubbing the wound, or using alcohol, spirits, ammonia, or urine will encourage the release of venom and should be avoided. A strange but effective method of treatment of stings is meat tenderizer which efficiently removes the nematocysts. Though often not available, a shower or bath as hot as can be tolerated can neutralize stings. However, if hypothermia is suspected this method may cause other serious complications.

Once deactivated, the stinging cells must be removed. This can be accomplished by picking off tentacles left on the body. First aid providers should be careful to use gloves or another readily available barrier device to prevent personal injury, and to follow standard universal precautions. After large pieces of the jellyfish are removed, shaving cream may be applied to the area and a knife edge, safety razor, or credit card may be used to take away any remaining nematocysts.

Beyond initial first aid, antihistamines such as diphenhydramine (Benadryl) may be used to control skin irritation (pruritus). To remove the venom in the skin, apply a paste of baking soda and water and apply a cloth covering on the sting. If possible, reapply paste every 15-20 minutes. Ice can be applied to stop the spread of venom until either of these is available.

Shark Finning

Shark finning is the controversial process of removing shark fins to provide the ingredients for the popular Asian dish of shark fin soup.

According to wildlife conservationists, much of the trade in sharks' fins is derived from fins cut from living sharks; this process is called finning. Because shark meat is worth much less, the finless and often still-living sharks are thrown back into the sea to make room on board the ship for more of the valuable fins. When returned to the ocean, the finless sharks, unable to move, either die from suffocation or are consumed by other sharks or animals.

However, according to Giam Choo Hoo, the longest serving member of the CITES Animals Committee, "The perception that it is common practice to kill sharks for only their fins - and to cut them off whilst the sharks are still alive - is wrong ... The vast majority of fins in the market are taken from sharks after their death." However, this discounting of an international phenomenon is disputed by extensive examination of fin sourcing and fisheries data as reported by Dr. Shelly Clarke in Ecology Letters. The first real-data study of sharks harvested for their valuable fins estimates that between 26 million and 73 million sharks are killed each year worldwide, three times higher than was reported originally by the United Nations.

Finning of living sharks on an industrial scale does occur and has been witnessed and photographed within the protected marine area of Costa Rica's Cocos Island National Park by the crew of the conservation vessel Ocean Warrior. The practice is featured in the documentary "Sharks: Stewards of the Reef", which contains footage from W. Australian waters and Central America and also examines the cultural, financial and ecological impacts of shark finning. This incident was also recorded by underwater photographer Richard Merritt who has witnessed finning of living sharks in Indonesia where he saw the immobile finless sharks lying still alive on the sea bed under the fishing boat. Finning has been witnessed and filmed within a protected marine area in the Raja Ampat islands of Indonesia.

Finning is vigorously opposed by animal welfare groups; both on moral grounds and also because it is listed as one of the causes for the rapid decline of global shark populations On the IUCN red list there are 39 species of elasmobranches (sharks and rays) listed as threatened species (Critically Endangered, Endangered or Vulnerable). It is estimated that 10–100 million sharks are slaughtered each year for their fins, with a median figure of 38 million. The industry is valued at US$1.2 billion; because of the lucrative profits, there are allegations of links to organized crime They also raise questions on the medical harm from the consumption of high levels of toxic mercury reportedly found in shark fins.

Numbers of some shark species have dropped as much as 80% over the past 60 years. Some organizations claim that shark fishing or bycatch (the unintentional capture of species by other fisheries) is the reason for the decline in the populations of some species and that the market for fins has very little impact – bycatch accounts for an estimated 50% of all sharks taken others that the market for shark fin soup is the main reason for the decline. Tommy Cheung, the legislator representing Hong Kong's catering sector, said: "I don't believe sharks are an endangered species. Some species of shark may be, but not all shark's fin comes from certain species. There are a lot of species that are plentiful." Since many countries do not allow shark finning there is no reliable count for the numbers taken in the shark fin trade and thus it is hard to prove the claims on either side of the argument. Sharks are caught for their fins and meat all over the world.

"Sharks are caught virtually all parts of the world. Despite the strongly declared objectives of the Fisheries Commission in

Brussels, there are very few restrictions on fishing for sharks in European waters. The meat of dogfishes, smoothhounds, catsharks, skates and rays is in high demand by European consumers...The situation in Canada and the United States is similar: the blue shark is sought after as a sport fish while the porbeagle, mako and spiny dogfish are part of the commercial fishery…the truth is this: Sharks will continue to be caught and killed on a wide scale by the more organized and sophisticated fishing nations...targeting shark's fin soup will not stop this accidental catch. The fins from these catches will be thrown away or turned into animal feed and fertilizers if shark's fin soup is shunned.

International Reaction

New laws have been passed to prevent finning; though much of the international waters continue to be unregulated. International fishing authorities are in the process of banning shark fishing (and finning) in the Atlantic Ocean and Mediterranean Sea. Finning is banned in the Eastern Pacific, but shark fishing and finning continues unabated in the rest of the Pacific and Indian Ocean.

Fisheries Management

Fisheries management is today often referred to as a governmental system of management rules based on defined objectives and a mix of management means to implement the rules, which is put in place by a system of monitoring control and surveillance (MCS). Modern fisheries management is most often based on biological arguments where the idea is to protect the biological resource in order to make a sustainable exploitation possible. The control of fisheries and fish production has been exercised in many places around the world for hundreds of years.

For example, the Maori people, residents of New Zealand for about the past 900 years, had strict rules in their traditional fishing activities about not taking more than could be eaten and about throwing back the first fish caught (as an offering to Tangaroa, god of the sea).

Another longstanding example is the North Norwegian fishery off the Lofoten islands, where a law has existed for more than 200 years to control fishing activity, in this case primarily motivated by problems occurring during periods of high density of fishers and fishing gear. To avoid gear collisions, gillnetters and longliners are separated and not allowed to fish in the same grounds south of Lofoten.

Governmental resource protection-based fisheries management is a relatively new idea, first developed for the North European fisheries after the first Overfishing Conference held in London in 1936. In 1957 the British fisheries researchers Ray Beverton and Sidney Holt published a seminal work on North Sea commercial species fisheries dynamics. The work was later (in the 1960s) used as a theoretical platform for the new management schemes set up in North European countries.

After some years away from the field of fisheries management, Ray Beverton reassessed his earlier work and in a paper given at the first World Fisheries Congress in Athens in 1992, he criticised some of the concepts that he had earlier laid out in "The Dynamics of Exploited Fish Populations" and expressed concern at the way his and Sydney Holt's work has been misinterpreted and misused by so many fishery biologists and managers during the previous 30 years. Nevertheless, the institutional foundation for modern fishery management had been laid.

Objectives

The political goal of resource use is often a weak part of the system of fisheries management, as conflicting objectives are often found.

Political objectives often found when exploiting a fish resource:

- Maximise sustainable biomass yield (see maximum sustainable yield)
- Maximise sustainable economic yield (see optimum sustainable yield)

- Secure and increase employment in certain regions
- Secure protein production and food supply
- Increase income from export
- Biological and economic yield

Management Rules

International agreements are required in order to regulate fisheries taking place in areas outside national control. The desire for agreement on this and other maritime issues led to the three conferences on the Law of the Sea, and ultimately to the treaty known as the United Nations Convention on the Law of the Sea (UNCLOS). Concepts such as exclusive economic zones (EEZ, extending 200 nautical miles (370 km) from the nation's coasts) allocate certain sovereign rights and responsibilities for resource management to individual countries.

There are a number of situations that need additional intergovernmental coordination. For example, in the Mediterranean Sea and other relatively narrow bodies of water, EEZ of 200 nautical miles are irrelevant, yet there are international waters beyond the 12-nautical-mile (22 km) line of coastal sovereignty. International agreements, therefore, must be worked out for fishery management in the international waters of the narrow sea. In the case of highly migratory species and straddling fish stocks, this sovereign responsibility must be exercised in collaboration with neighbouring coastal states and fishing entities, usually through the medium of an intergovernmental regional organisation set up for the purpose of coordinating the management of that stock.

UNCLOS does not prescribe precisely how fisheries that occur solely in international waters should be managed, and there are several new fisheries (such as high seas bottom trawling fisheries) that are not yet subject to international agreement across their entire range. Both of these issues came to a head within the United Nations in 2004 and the UN General Assembly issued a resolution on Fisheries in November 2004 which set the scene for the further development of international fisheries management law.

Fisheries objectives need to be expressed in concrete management rules. In most countries the management rules today should be based on the internationally agreed, albeit non-binding, standard Code of Conduct for Responsible Fisheries, agreed at an FAO session in 1995. The precautionary approach prescribed here is also implemented in concrete management rules as minimum spawning biomass, maximum fishing mortality rates, etc.

Management Mechanisms

When it comes to controlling the activities of individual fishers or fishing operations (vessels or companies), available management means can be sorted into four categories:

Taxation on input; vessel licensing	Taxation on output; restrictions on catching techniques
Limited entry control	Catch quota and technical regulation

The top row represents indirect methods while the bottom row represents direct methods of regulation. vessel monitoring systems, patrol vessels and aircraft, and observers aboard fishing vessels are examples of direct regulatory methods. The left column shows input controls and the right column output controls.

Many countries have set up Ministries and Government Departments, named "Ministry of Fisheries" or similar, controlling aspects of fisheries within their exclusive economic zones.

Technical regulation of fishing may include:

- the prohibition of fishing with the use of mechanical devices such as bows and arrows, and spears, or firearms
- the prohibition of fishing with nets
- the prohibition of fishing with bait
- snagging of fish

- regulation of fish traps
- restrictions on the number of poles or lines per fisherman

Bottom Trawling

Bottom trawling is trawling (towing a trawl, which is a fishing net) along the sea floor.

The scientific community divides bottom trawling into benthic trawling and demersal trawling. Benthic trawling is towing a net at the very bottom of the ocean and demersal trawling is towing a net just above the benthic zone.

Bottom trawling can be contrasted with midwater trawling (also known as pelagic trawling), where a net is towed higher in the water column. Midwater trawling catches pelagic fish such as anchovies, shrimp, tuna and mackerel, whereas bottom trawling targets both bottom living fish (groundfish) and semi-pelagic fish such as cod, squid, halibut and rockfish.

Trawling is done by a trawler, which can be a small open boat with only 30 hp or a large factory trawler with 10,000 hp (7,500 kW). Bottom trawling can be carried out by one trawler or by two trawlers fishing cooperatively (pair trawling).

An early reference to fishery conservation measures comes from a complaint about a form of trawling dating from the 14th century, during the reign of Edward III. A petition was presented to Parliament in 1376 calling for the prohibition of a "subtlety contrived instrument called the *wondyrchoum*". This was an early beam trawl with a wooden beam, and consisted of a net 6m (18 ft) long and 3m (l0 ft.) wide, "of so small a mesh, no manner of fish, however small, entering within it can pass out and is compelled to remain therein and be taken...by means of which instrument the fishermen aforesaid take so great abundance of small fish aforesaid, that they know not what to do with them, but feed and fatten the pigs with them, to the great damage of the whole commons of the kingdom, and the destruction of the fisheries in like places, for which they pray remedy."

Another source describes the wondyrchoun as "three fathom long and ten mens' feet wide, and that it had a beam ten feet long, at the end of which were two frames formed like a colerake, that a leaded rope weighted with a great many stones was fixed on the lower part of the net between the two frames, and that another rope was fixed with nails on the upper part of the beam, so that the fish entering the space between the beam and the lower net were caught. The net had maskes of the length and breadth of two men's thumbs"

The response from the Crown was to "let Commission be made by qualified persons to inquire and certify on the truth of this allegation, and thereon let right be done in the Court of Chancery". Thus, already back in the Middle Ages, basic arguments about three of the most sensitive current issues surrounding trawling - the effect of trawling on the wider environment, the use of small mesh size, and of industrial fishing for animal feed - were already being raised.

Although trawl nets were used by sailing vessels up to the 19th century, it was only with the development of steam power and the diesel engine that bottom trawling became a widely used method of fishing.

English commissions in the 19th century determined that there should be no limitation on trawling. They believed that bottom trawling, like tilling of land, actually increased production. As evidence, they noted that a second trawler would often follow a first trawler, and that the second trawler would often harvest even more fish than the first. The reason for this peculiarity is that the destruction caused by the first trawl resulted in many dead and dying organisms, which temporarily attracted a large number of additional species to feed on this moribund mass.

Bottom trawling has been widely implicated in the population collapse of a variety of fish species, locally and worldwide, including orange roughy, barndoor skate, shark, and many others.

The design requirements of a bottom trawl are relatively simple, a mechanism for keeping the mouth of the net open in horizontal and vertical dimensions, a "body" of net which guides fish inwards, and a "cod-end" of a suitable mesh size, where the fish are collected. The size and design of net used is determined by the species being targeted, the engine power and design of the fishing vessel and locally enforced regulations.

The simplest method of bottom trawling, the mouth of the net is held open by a solid metal beam, attached to two "shoes", which are solid metal plates, welded to the ends of the beam, which slide over and disturb the seabed. This method is mainly used on smaller vessels, fishing for flatfish or prawns, relatively close inshore.

Otter Trawling

Otter trawling derives its name from the large rectangular otter boards which are used to keep the mouth of the trawl net open. Otter boards are made of timber or steel and are positioned in such a way that the hydrodynamic forces, acting on them when the net is towed along the seabed, pushes them outwards and prevents the mouth of the net from closing. They also act like a plough, digging up to 15 cm into the seabed, creating a turbid cloud, and scaring fish towards the net mouth. The net is held open vertically on an otter trawl by floats and/or kites attached to the "headline" (the rope which runs along the upper mouth of the net), and weighted "bobbins" attached to the "foot rope" (the rope which runs along the lower mouth of the net). These bobbins vary in their design depending on the roughness of the sea bed which is being fished, varying from small rubber discs for very smooth, sandy ground, to large metal balls, up to 0.5 m in diameter for very rough ground. These bobbins can also be designed to lift the net off the seabed when they hit an obstacle. These are known as "rock-hopper" gears.

Body of the Trawl

The body of the trawl is funnel-like, wide at its "mouth" and narrowing towards the codend, and usually is fitted with wings of netting at the both sides of the mouth. It is long enough to assure adequate flow of water and prevent fish from escaping the net, after having been caught. It is made of diamond-meshed netting, the size of the meshes decreasing from the front of the net towards the codend. Into the body, fish and turtle escape devices can be fitted. These can be simple structures like "square mesh panels", which are easier for smaller fish to pass through, or more complicated devices, such as bycatch grills.

The business end of the net, the cod end is where fish are finally "caught". The size of mesh in the cod end is a determinant of the size of fish which the net catches. Consequently, regulation of mesh size is a common way of managing mortality of juvenile fishes in trawl nets.

How Trawls Work

The idea that fish are passively "scooped up" is commonly held, and has been since trawling was first developed, but has been revealed to be erroneous. Since the development of scuba diving equipment and cheap video cameras it has been possible to directly observe the processes that occur when a trawl is towed along the seabed.

The trawl doors disturb the sea bed, create a cloud of muddy water which hides the oncoming trawl net and generates a noise which attracts fish. The fish begin to swim in front of the net mouth, but do not seem to be distressed by it. As the trawl continues along the seabed, fish begin to tire and slip backwards into the net. Finally, the fish become exhausted and drop back, into the "cod end" and are caught. The speed that the trawl is towed at depends on the swimming speed of the species which is being targeted and the exact gear that is being used, but for most demersal species, a speed of around 4 knots (7 km/h) is appropriate.

Bottom fishing has operated for over a century on heavily fished grounds such as the North Sea and Grand Banks. Although overfishing has caused huge ecological changes to the fish community on the Grand Banks, concern has been raised recently about the damage which benthic trawling inflicts upon seabed communities. A species of particular concern is the slow growing, deep water coral *Lophelia pertusa*. This species is home to a diverse community of deep sea organisms, but is easily damaged by fishing gear. On November 18, 2004 the United Nations General Assembly urged nations to consider temporary bans on high seas bottom trawling.

Bottom trawling stirs up the sediment at the bottom of the sea. The suspended solid plumes can drift with the current for tens of kilometres from the source of the trawling. These plumes introduce a turbidity which decreases light levels at the bottom and can affect kelp reproduction.

Ocean sediments are the sink for many persistent organic pollutants, usually lipophilic pollutants like DDT, PCB and PAH Bottom trawling mixes these pollutants into the plankton ecology where they can move back up the food chain and into our food supply.

Phosphorus is often found in high concentration in soft shallow sediments Resuspending nutrient solids like these can introduce oxygen demand into the water column, and result in oxygen deficient dead zones.

Even in areas where the bottom sediments are ancient, bottom trawling, by reintroducing the sediment into the water column, can create harmful algae blooms. More suspended solids are introduced into the oceans from bottom trawling than any other man-made source.

Current Restrictions

Today, some countries regulate bottom trawling within their jurisdictions:

- The United States National Oceanic and Atmospheric Administration banned bottom trawling off most of its Pacific coast in early 2006 and has restricted the practice severely off its other coasts as well. This Federal regulation affects areas between 3-300 miles from the coast (areas within 3 miles (4.8 km) of the coast are State regulated).
- The Council of the European Union in 2004 applied "a precautionary approach" and closed the sensitive Darwin Mounds off Scotland to bottom trawling.
- In 2005, the FAO's General Fisheries Commission for the Mediterranean (GFCM) banned bottom trawling below 1000 metres and, in January 2006, completely closed ecologically sensitive areas off Italy, Cyprus, and Egypt to all bottom trawling.

- Norway first recognized in 1999 that trawling had caused significant damage to its cold-water lophelia corals. Norway has since established a program to determine the location of cold-water corals within its EEZ so as to quickly close those areas to bottom trawling.
- Canada has acted to protect vulnerable coral reef ecosystems from bottom trawling off Nova Scotia. The Northeast Channel was protected by a fisheries closure in 2002, and the Gully area was protected by its designation as a Marine Protected Area (MPA) in 2004.
- Australia in 1999 established the Tasmanian Seamounts Marine Reserve to prohibit bottom trawling in the south Tasman Sea. Australia also prohibits bottom trawling in The Great Australian Bight Marine Park near Ceduna off South Australia. In 2004, Australia established the world's largest marine protected area in the Great Barrier Reef Marine Park where fishing and other extractive activities are prohibited.
- New Zealand in 2001 closed 19 seamounts within its EEZ to bottom trawling, including in the Chatham Rise, sub-Antarctic waters, and off the east and west coasts of the North Island. New Zealand Fisheries Minister Jim Anderton announced on 14th February 2006 that a draft agreement had been reached with fishing companies to ban bottom trawling in 30 percent of New Zealand's exclusive economic zone, an area of about 1.2 million km^2 reaching from sub-Antarctic waters to sub-tropical ones. But only a small fraction of the area proposed for protection will cover areas actually vulnerable to bottom trawling.
- Palau has banned all bottom trawling within its jurisdiction and by any Palauan or Palauan corporation anywhere in the world.
- The President of Kiribati, Anote Tong, announced in early 2006 the formation of the world's first deep sea marine reserve area. This measure—the Phoenix Islands Protected Area—creates the world's third largest marine protected area and may protect deep sea corals, fish, and seamounts

from bottom trawling. However, the actual boundaries of this reserve and what harvest limitations may occur therein have not been detailed. Moreover, Kiribati currently has only 1 patrol boat to monitor this proposed region.

Lack of Regulation

Beyond national jurisdictions, most bottom trawling is unregulated either because there is no Regional Fisheries Management Organization (RFMO) with competence to regulate, or else what RFMOs that do exist have not actually regulated. The major exception to this is in the Antarctic region, where the Convention for the Conservation of Antarctic Marine Living Resources regime has instituted extensive bottom trawling restrictions. The North East Atlantic Fisheries Commission (NEAFC) also recently closed four seamounts and part of the mid-Atlantic Ridge from all fishing, including bottom trawling, for three years. This still leaves most of international waters completely without bottom trawl regulation.

As of May 2007 the area managed under the South Pacific Regional Fisheries Management Organisation (SPRFMO) has gained a new level of protection. All countries fishing in the region (accounting for about 25 percent of the global ocean) agreed to exclude bottom trawling on high seas areas where vulnerable ecosystems are likely or known to occur until a specific impact assessment is undertaken and precautionary measures have been are implemented. Also observers will be required on all high seas bottom trawlers to ensure enforcement of the regulations.

10

Marine Microbes

Introduction

The term 'Marine microbes' encompasses all microscopic organisms generally found in saltwater. Most micro-organisms are acellular and fall into the major categories of viruses, prokaryotes ('bacteria'), and protists, groups which differ considerably in biological characteristics. While representatives of these groups are found in virtually everywhere in marine waters and they play nearly every ecological role imaginable, their most important function is that they form the base of the food chain in marine ecosystems.

Viruses

Well-known to us as disease-causing agents, viruses are deceivigly simple organisms, little more than some nucleic acid within a protein container. They are 'parasitic particles' most about 40 nanometers in size. Viruses attach themselves to a living cell and inject a bit of nucleic acid into the cell; the injected nucleic acid directs the living cell to produce viruses. Generally, viruses are 'host-specific' only attacking or pirating a single species. They are very abundant in the sea; a tablespoon of seawater, 5 ml, commonly contains about 50 million viruses. As bacteria (or prokaryotes) are the most common potential host organisms in the sea, most viruses are bacteriophages (bacteria-consuming).

Prokaryotes

Prokaryotes are organisms without a distinct nucleus (their DNA is not bound within a membrane sac inside the cell). Typically, they are from 0.5 - 2 micrometers in size. Until recently known simply as 'bacteria', the 2 main groups recognized today are archaeabacteria and eubacteria which differ in the composition of their cell membranes. There appear to be no fundamental differences in the physiology or ecological roles played by the two types of prokaryotes but archaeabacteria appear do often to inhabit relatively extreme habitats such as the deep sea.

Most bacteria obtain energy by either absorbing marine dissolved organic matter through their cell membranes-osmotrophy (literally feeding through 'osmosis' in fact the material taken up is simply not obviously particulate, osmosis has little to do with the mechanisms used). However, some rely on sunlight and photosynthesis or the energy contained in some inorganic compounds (autotrophy or self-feeding). They are found in every environment, from sea ice at the poles to deep-sea hydrothermal vents. In seawater typical concentrations are about a million per ml or 5 million in a tablespoon.

Protists are eukaryotic, possessing a membrane-bound nucleus, but are single-celled or acellular organisms. The group includes all eukaryotic organisms which are not multi-cellular. Thus, it is a group of organisms united more by what they are not - multicellular - then by ancestry or common ecological characteristics. Marine protists typically range in size from 2 to 200 micrometers. Whereas viruses are parasites, and prokaryotes are osmotrophs or autotrophs, marine protist provide examples of these distinct life-styles as well as certain combinations of strategies.

The different types are found in different concentrations. Protists which have chloroplasts, allowing them to perform photosynthesis thus act as autotrophs, are generally found in the highest concentrations. The larger forms (10-200 micrometers in size) include diatoms and many dinoflagellates. The most abundant are small (1-10 micrometers long) flagellates.

Autotrophic protists are restricted to the upper sunlit portion of the seas and found in abundances of a thousand per ml for the small flagellates. While they have few morphological characteristics allowing us to distinguish species, recent genetic studies suggest that small marine flagellates may be a very diverse group of organisms. Larger autrophic protists such as diatoms and dinoflagellates typically occur in concentrations of about one cell per ml.

Protists which rely on aquiring pre-formed organic matter are heterotrophic. Usually in surface waters there are about a thousand per ml of small flagellates which feed on bacteria (both autotrophic and heterotrophic prokaryotes) and 1 or 2 ciliates, oligotrichs) and tintinnids or heterotrophic dinoflagellates which feed on autotrophic protists. Besides these two large, common life-styles there are parasitic protists as well 'mixotrophic' protists. Mixotrophic protists use both photosynthesis from chloroplasts as well as feeding on pre-formed organic matter, often in the form of other protists. Some protist species retain and use the chloroplasts in the prey they eat while other protists harbor symbionts, entire autotrophic bacteria or protists.

Ecological Roles of Marine Microbes

Primary production is 'first production' - the creation of organic matter. Usually it refers to the transformation, or fixation, of inorganic carbon into simple sugars using solar energy through photosynthesis. On land, the primary producers take the form of grasses, bushes, and trees and these plants are usually the most visible of all organisms within a given locality. However, in the sea (with the exception of coastal areas with seagrasses & seaweeds) the primary producers appear invisible because they microscopic and the organisms we see are high up in the food chain. The primary producers are microbes. This is not only in open water areas where the plants are in the form of the plankton (the plant plankton or phytoplankton) but it also true of many shallow areas.

Among the prokaryotes, the most abundant and important primary producers are species of the genera Synechococcus and Prochlorococcus. They are capable of reproducing once per day and form most of the 'plant' biomass in many areas of the open sea, especially in the tropics. As these cells are small (about a micrometer across) the most likely consumers of Synechococcus or Prochlorococcus are flagellate and ciliate protists.

In most coastal zones, protists form the bulk of the phytoplankton. Diatoms , dinoflagellates , and many different types of flagellates are responsible for most of the primary production. Many are large enough (> 100 micrometer) to be consumed by filter-feeding fish such as anchovies and sardines. However, throughout most of the seas, protist primary producers are small flagellates (2-10 micrometers) and fed upon by other protists, typically ciliates.

Consumers of plants or primary producers, are herbivores and the production (increases in numbers or individual mass) of herbivores is called secondary production. Among marine microbes, consumers of primary producers are those which feed on autotrophic prokaryotes or autotrophic protists. Thus, the viruses which attack the autotrophic prokaryotes Synechococcus, the bacteria which absorb dissolved organic excreted by autotrophic protists such as diatoms and dinoflagellates, and the protists such as ciliates, radiolarians which feed on autotrophic protists are all consumers of primary production. However, these simple relationships exist alongside many others because among marine microbes there is not a food chain but rather a web.

Thinking in terms of food chains, more often than not marine microbes are not exactly akin to plant (phytoplankton) nor animal (zooplankton). Furthermore, relationships between different microbes are usually neither direct nor exclusive. For example, the dissolved organic matter absorbed by a bacterium is likely a mixture of that excreted by a primary producer and some from the viral lysis of another bacterium as well the excreta of yet another organism that fed on a herbivore or a primary producer. Similarly, among protists, a radiolarian may capture and ingest, more or less indifferently, a bacterium, an autotrophic flagellate, a herbivorous oligotrich ciliate, or another radiolarian While the ecological roles are not often clear cut among marine microbes, the rest of the marine food web ultimately depends on the microbial community.

Marine Biology

Marine biology is the scientific study of living organisms in the ocean or other marine or brackish bodies of water. Given that in biology many phyla, families and genera have some species that live in the sea and others that live on land, marine biology classifies species based on the environment rather than on taxonomy. Marine biology differs from marine ecology as marine ecology is focused on how organisms interact with each other and environment and biology is the study of the animal it self.

Marine life is a vast resource, providing food, medicine, and raw materials, in addition to helping to support recreation and tourism all over the world. At a fundamental level, marine life helps determine the very nature of our planet. Marine organisms contribute significantly to the oxygen cycle, and are involved in the regulation of the earth's climate. Shorelines are in part shaped and protected by marine life, and some marine organisms even help create new land.

Marine biology covers a great deal, from the microscopic, including most zooplankton and phytoplankton, where zooplankton can be as small as 0.02 micrometers or as big as 2 metres in the case of the sunfish to the huge cetaceans (whales) which reach up to a reported 48 meters (125 feet) in length.

The habitats studied by marine biology include everything from the tiny layers of surface water in which organisms and abiotic items may be trapped in surface tension between the ocean and atmosphere, to the depths of the abyssal trenches, sometimes 10,000 meters or more beneath the surface of the ocean. It studies habitats such as coral reefs, kelp forests, tidepools, muddy, sandy and rocky bottoms, and the open ocean (pelagic) zone, where solid objects are rare and the surface of the water is the only visible boundary.

A large amount of all life on Earth exists in the oceans. Exactly how large the proportion is still unknown. While the oceans comprise about 71% of the Earth's surface, due to their depth they encompass about 300 times the habitable volume of the terrestrial habitats on Earth.

Many species are economically important to humans, including food fish. It is also becoming understood that the well-being of marine organisms and other organisms are linked in very fundamental ways. The human body of knowledge regarding the relationship between life in the sea and important cycles is rapidly growing. These cycles include those of matter (such as the carbon cycle) and of air (such as Earth's respiration, and movement of energy through ecosystems). Large areas beneath the ocean surface still remain effectively unexplored.

Subfields

The marine ecosystem is large, and thus there are many subfields of marine biology. Most involve studying specializations of particular species (i.e. phycology, invertebrate zoology and ichthyology). Other subfields study the physical effects of continual immersion in sea water and the ocean in general, adaptation to a salty environment, and the effects of changing various oceanic properties on marine life. A subfield of marine biology studies the relationships between oceans and ocean life, and global warming and environmental issues (such as carbon dioxide displacement).

Recent marine biotechnology has focused largely on marine biomolecules, especially proteins, that may have uses in medicine or engineering. Marine environments are the home to many exotic biological materials that may inspire biomimetic materials. Marine biology is a branch of oceanography and is closely linked to biology. It also encompasses many ideas from ecology. Fisheries science and marine conservation can be considered partial offshoots of marine biology.

Microscopic Life

Microscopic life undersea is incredibly diverse and still poorly understood. For example, the role of viruses in marine ecosystems is barely being explored even in the beginning of the 21st century.

The role of phytoplankton is better understood due to their critical position as the most numerous primary producers on Earth. Phytoplankton are categorized into cyanobacteria (also called blue-green algae/bacteria), various types of algae (red, green, brown, and yellow-green), diatoms, dinoflagellates, euglenoids, coccolithophorids, cryptomonads, chrysophytes, chlorophytes, prasinophytes, and silicoflagellates.

Zooplankton tend to be somewhat larger, and not all are microscopic. Many Protozoa are zooplankton, including dinoflagellates, zooflagellates, foraminiferans, and radiolarians. Some of these (such as dinoflaggelates) are also phytoplankton; the plant/animal distinction often breaks down in very small organisms. Other zooplankton include cnidarians, ctenophores, chaetognaths, molluscs, arthropods, urochordates, and annelids such as polychaetes. Many larger animals begin their life as zooplankton before they become large enough to take their familiar forms. Two examples are fish larvae and sea stars (also called starfish).

Plants and Algae

Plant life is relatively rare undersea. Most of the niche occupied by sub plants on land is actually occupied by macroscopic algae in the ocean, such as *Sargassum* and kelp, which are commonly known as seaweeds that create kelp forests. The non algae plants that do survive in the sea are often found in shallow waters, such as the seagrasses (examples of which are eelgrass, *Zostera*, and turtle grass, *Thalassia*). These plants have adapted to the high salinity of the ocean environment. The intertidal zone is also a good place to find plant life in the sea, where mangroves or cordgrass or beach grass might grow. Sea kelp is very important to small sea creatures because the creatures can hide from predators. Eel grass is the most important. It is where hairing and other small fish live to escape from preditors.

Marine Invertebrates

As on land, invertebrates make up a huge portion of all life in the sea. Invertebrate sea life includes Cnidaria such as jellyfish and sea anemones; Ctenophora; sea worms including the phyla Platyhelminthes, Nemertea, Annelida, Sipuncula, Echiura, Chaetognatha, and the Phoronida; Mollusca including shellfish, squid, octopus; Crustacea; Porifera; Bryozoa; Echinodermata including starfish; and Urochordete - sea squirts or tunicates.

Fish

Fish have evolved very different biological functions from other large organisms. Fish anatomy includes a two-chambered heart, operculum, secretory cells that produce mucous, swim bladder, scales, fins, lips and eyes. Fish breathe by extracting oxygen from water through their gills. Fins propel and stabilize the fish in the water.

Well known fish include: sardines, anchovy, ling cod, clownfish (also known as anemonefish), and bottom fish which include halibut or ling cod. Predators include sharks and barracuda.

Reptiles

Reptiles which inhabit or frequent the sea include sea turtles, Marine Iguana, sea snakes, and Saltwater Crocodiles. Most extant marine reptiles, except for some sea snakes are oviparous and need to return to land to lay their eggs. Thus most species, excepting sea turtles, live on or near land rather than in the ocean. Some extinct marine reptiles, such as ichthyosaurs, evolved to be viviparous and had no requirement to return to land.

Seabirds

Seabirds are species of birds adapted to living in the marine environment, examples including albatross, penguins, gannets, and auks. Although they spend most of their lives in the ocean, species such as gulls can often be found thousands of miles inland.

Reefs

Reefs comprise some of the densest and most diverse habitats in the world. The best-known types of reefs are tropical coral reefs which exist in most tropical waters; however, reefs can also exist in cold water. Reefs are built up by corals and other calcium-depositing animals, usually on top of a rocky outcrop on the ocean floor. Reefs can also grow on other surfaces, which has made it possible to create artificial reefs. Coral reefs also support a huge community of life, including the corals themselves, their symbiotic zooxanthellae, tropical fish and many other organisms.

Much attention in marine biology is focused on coral reefs and the El Niño weather phenomenon. In 1998, coral reefs experienced a "once in a thousand years" bleaching event, in which vast expanses of reefs across the Earth died because sea surface temperatures rose well above normal. Some reefs are recovering, but scientists say that 58% of the world's coral reefs are now endangered and predict that global warming could exacerbate this trend.

Deep Sea and Trenches

The deepest recorded oceanic trenches measure to date is the Mariana Trench, near the Philippines, in the Pacific Ocean at 10924 m (35838 ft). At such depths, water pressure is extreme and there is no sunlight, but some life still exists. Small flounder (family Soleidae) fish and shrimp were seen by the American crew of the bathyscaphe *Trieste* when it dove to the bottom in 1960.

Other notable oceanic trenches include Monterey Canyon, in the eastern Pacific, the Tonga Trench in the southwest at 10,882 m (35,702 ft), the Philippine Trench, the Puerto Rico Trench at 8605 m (28232 ft), the Romanche Trench at 7760 m (24450 ft), Fram Basin in the Arctic Ocean at 4665 m (15305 ft), the Java Trench at 7450 m (24442 ft), and the South Sandwich Trench at 7235 m (23737 ft).

In general, the deep sea is considered to start at the aphotic zone, the point where sunlight loses its power of transference through the water. Many life forms that live at these depths have the ability to create their own light.

Much life centers on seamounts that rise from the deeps, where fish and other sea life congregate to spawn and feed. Hydrothermal vents along the mid-ocean ridge spreading centers act as oases, as do their opposites, cold seeps. Such places support unique biomes and many new microbes and other lifeforms have been discovered at these locations.

Open Ocean

The great expanse of open ocean habitat is huge, and many species can be found passing through it and living in it. The term "open ocean" usually is meant to refer to the vast stretches of water between points of land, or between undersea mounts. Contrary to popular notions the open ocean is often not the place where marine animals spend the majority of their lives. Most species simply pass through the open ocean on their ways to other places. Larger species are the main ongoing inhabitants.

Intertidal and Shore

Intertidal zones, those areas close to shore, are constantly being exposed and covered by the ocean's tides. A huge array of life lives within this zone.

Shore habitats span from the upper intertidal zones to the area where land vegetation takes prominence. It can be underwater anywhere from daily to very infrequently. Many species here are scavengers, living off of sea life that is washed up on the shore. Many land animals also make much use of the shore and intertidal habitats. A subgroup of organisms in this habitat bores and grinds exposed rock through the process of bioerosion.

An active research topic in marine biology is to discover and map the life cycles of various species and where they spend their time. Marine biologists study how the ocean currents, tides and many other oceanic factors affect ocean lifeforms, including their growth, distribution and well-being. This has only recently become technically feasible with advances in GPS and newer underwater visual devices.

Most ocean life breeds in specific places, nests or not in others, spends time as juveniles in still others, and in maturity in yet others. Scientists know little about where many species spent different parts of their life cycles. For example, it is still largely unknown where sea turtles travel. Tracking devices do not work for some life forms, and the ocean is not friendly to technology.

11

Marine Mammals

Introduction

Marine mammals are a diverse group of roughly 120 species of mammal that are primarily ocean-dwelling or depend on the ocean for food. They include the cetaceans (whales, dolphins, and porpoises), the sirenians (manatees and dugong), the pinnipeds (true seals, eared seals and walrus), and several otters (the sea otter and marine otter). The polar bear is also usually grouped with the marine mammals.

Marine mammals evolved from land dwelling ancestors and share several adaptive features for life at sea such as generally large size, hydrodynamic body shapes, modified appendages and various thermoregulatory adaptations. Different species are, however, adapted to marine life to varying degrees. The most fully adapted are the cetaceans and the sirenians, whose entire life cycle takes place under water, whereas the other groups spend at least some time on land.

Despite the fact that marine mammals are highly recognizable charismatic megafauna, many populations are vulnerable or endangered due to a history of commercial exploitation for blubber, meat, ivory and fur. Most species are currently protected from commercial exploitation.

ADAPTATIONS

Since mammals originally evolved on land, their spines are optimized for running, allowing for up-and-down but only little sideways motion. Therefore, marine mammals typically swim by moving their spine up and down. By contrast, fish normally swim by moving their spine sideways. For this reason, fish mostly have vertical caudal (tail) fins, while marine mammals have horizontal caudal fins.

Some of the primary differences between marine mammals and other marine life are:

- Marine mammals breathe air, while most other marine animals extract oxygen from water.
- Marine mammals have hair. Cetaceans have little or no hair, usually a very few bristles retained around the head or mouth. All members of the Carnivora have a coat of fur or hair, but it is far thicker and more important for thermoregulation in sea otters and polar bears than in seals or sea lions. Thick layers of fur contribute to drag while swimming, and slow down a swimming mammal, giving it a disadvantage in speed.
- Marine mammals have thick layers of blubber used to insulate their bodies and prevent heat loss. Sea otters and polar bears are exceptions, relying more on fur and behavior to stave off hypothermia.
- Marine mammals give birth. Most marine mammals give birth to one calf or pup at a time.
- Marine mammals feed off milk as young. Maternal care is extremely important to the survival of offspring that need to develop a thick insulating layer of blubber. The milk from the mammary glands of marine mammals often exceeds 40-50% fat content to support the development of blubber in the young.
- Marine mammals maintain a high internal body temperature. Unlike most other marine life, marine mammals carefully maintain a core temperature much

higher than their environment. Blubber, thick coats of fur, bubbles of air between skin and water, countercurrent exchange, and behaviours such as hauling out, are all adaptations that aid marine mammals in retention of body heat.

The polar bear spends a large portion of its time in a marine environment, albeit a frozen one. When it does swim in the open sea it is extremely proficient and has been shown to cover 74 km in a day. For these reasons, some scientists regard it as a marine mammal.

Considerable research has been conducted on the incidence of diseases that afflict marine mammals in the marine environment. This work has addressed leptospirosis, phocine herpesvirus, neurological diseases, toxicology and other pathologies affecting marine mammals. Entire research organizations have developed such as the Marine Mammal Center to focus upon the rehabilitation and research functions of marine mammals.

CETACEA

The order Cetacea includes whales, dolphins and porpoises. *Cetus* is Latin and is used in biological names to mean "whale"; its original meaning, "large sea animal", was more general. It comes from Ancient Greek (*ketos*), meaning "whale" or "any huge fish or sea monster". In Greek mythology the monster Perseus defeated was called Ceto, which is depicted by the constellation of Cetus. Cetology is the branch of marine science associated with the study of cetaceans.

Cetaceans are the mammals most fully adapted to aquatic life. Their body is fusiform (spindle-shaped). The forelimbs are modified into flippers. The tiny hindlimbs are vestigial; they do not attach to the backbone and are hidden within the body. The tail has horizontal flukes. Cetaceans are nearly hairless, and are insulated by a thick layer of blubber.. As a group, they are noted for their high intelligence.

The order Cetacea contains about ninety species, all marine except for four species of freshwater dolphins. The order is divided into two suborders, Mysticeti (baleen whales) and Odontoceti (toothed whales, which includes dolphins and porpoises). The species range in size from the Commerson's Dolphin and Tucuxi to the Blue Whale, the world's largest ever animal.

Respiration, Vision, Hearing and Echolocation

As mammals, cetaceans need to breathe air. Because of this, they need to come to the water's surface to exhale carbon dioxide and inhale a fresh supply of oxygen. During diving, a muscular action closes the blowholes (nostrils), which remain closed until the cetacean next breaks the surface; when it surfaces, the muscles open the blowholes and warm air is exhaled.

Cetaceans' blowholes have evolved to a position on top of the head, allowing more time to expel stale air and inhale fresh air. When the stale air, warmed from the lungs, is exhaled, it condenses as it meets the cold air outside. As with a terrestrial mammal breathing out on a cold day, a small cloud of 'steam' appears. This is called the 'blow' or 'spout' and is different in terms of shape, angle and height, for each cetacean species. Cetaceans can be identified at a distance, using this characteristic, by experienced whalers or whale-watchers.

Cetaceans can go underwater for much longer periods of time than other mammals. Their duration under water varies greatly between species due to large physiological differences between many members of this Order. There are two studied[*citation needed*] advantages of cetacean physiology that let this Order (and other marine mammals) forage underwater for extended periods of time without breathing at the water surface.

Myoglobin concentrations in skeletal muscle of mammals have much variation. A New Zealand white rabbit has 0.08±/-0.06 g (in a 100 g Wet muscle) of myoglobin, whereas a Northern Bottlenose Whale has 6.34 g (in a 100 g wet muscle) of myoglobin. Myoglobin, by nature, has a higher affinity to oxygen than hemoglobin. That is, myoglobin retains oxygen molecules better than hemoglobin. Therefore, it is useful to have higher concentrations of myoglobin when needed and there is no oxygen available for re-uptake. The higher the myoglobin concentration in cetacean skeletal muscle, the longer they can stay underwater and forage.

Increased body size is another way of elongating dive duration of large cetaceans. This is true because of two considered aspects. An increase in body size means that there is increase in muscle mass, therefore, increase in muscle oxygen stores. Another aspect is the universal correlation of mass and metabolic rate (Kleiber's law). In layman's terms, Kleiber's law states that the metabolic rate of a large animal is slower than a small animal per unit mass. From this we can conclude that larger animals will use up less oxygen than smaller animals (per mass unit).

The cetacean's eyes are set well back and to either side of its huge head. This means that cetaceans with pointed 'beaks' (such as dolphins) have good binocular vision forward and downward but others, with blunt heads (such as the Sperm Whale), can see either side but not directly ahead or directly behind. Tear glands secrete greasy tears, which protect the eyes from the salt in the water. Cetaceans also have an almost spherical lens in their eyes, which is most efficient at focusing what little light there is in the deep waters. Cetaceans make up for their generally quite poor vision (with the exception of the dolphin) with excellent hearing.

As with the eyes, the cetacean's ears are also small. Life in the sea accounts for the cetacean's loss of its external ears, whose function is to collect airborne sound waves and focus them in order for them to become strong enough to hear well. However, water is a better conductor of sound than air, so the external ear was no longer needed: it is no more than a tiny hole in the skin, just behind the eye. The inner ear, however, has become so well developed that the cetacean can not only hear sounds dozens of miles away, but it can also discern from which direction the sound comes.

Some cetaceans are capable of echolocation. Many toothed whales emit clicks similar to those in echolocation, but it has not been demonstrated that they echolocate. Mysticeti have little need of echolocation, as they prey upon small fish that would be impractical to locate with echolocation. Some members of Odontoceti, such as dolphins and porpoises, do perform echolocation. These cetaceans use sound in the same way as bats—they emit a sound (called a click), which then bounces off an object and returns to them. From this, cetaceans can discern the size, shape, surface characteristics and movement of the object, as well as how far away it is. With this ability cetaceans can search for, chase and catch fast-swimming prey in total darkness. Echolocation is so advanced in most Odontoceti that they can distinguish between prey and non-prey (such as humans or boats); captive cetaceans can be trained to distinguish between, for example, balls of different sizes or shapes.

Cetaceans also use sound to communicate, whether it be groans, moans, whistles, clicks or the complex 'singing' of the Humpback Whale.

Feeding

When it comes to food and feeding, cetaceans can be separated into two distinct groups. The toothed whales, Odontoceti like the Sperm Whale, Beluga, dolphins and porpoises, usually have lots of teeth that they use for catching fish, squid or other marine life. They do not chew their food, but swallow it whole. In the rare cases that they catch large prey, as when the Orca (*Orcinus orca*) catches a seal, they tear chunks off it that in turn are swallowed whole.

The baleen whales or Mysticeti do not have teeth. Instead they have plates made of keratin (the same substance as human fingernails) which hang down from the upper jaw. These plates act like a giant filter, straining small animals (such as krill and fish) from the seawater. Cetaceans included in this group include the Blue Whale, the Humpback Whale, the Bowhead Whale and the two minke whale species.

Not all Mysticeti feed on plankton: the larger whales tend to eat small shoaling fish, such as herrings and sardines, called micronecton. One species of Mysticeti, the Gray Whale (*Eschrichtius robustus*), is a benthic feeder, primarily eating sea floor crustaceans.

Mammalian Nature

Cetaceans are mammals, that is, members of the class Mammalia. The closest living relative of cetaceans is the hippopotamus.

As mammals, cetaceans have characteristics that are common to all mammals: they are warm-blooded, breathe in air through their lungs, bear their young alive and suckle them on their own milk, and have hair, although very little of it.

Another way of discerning a cetacean from a fish is by the shape of the tail. The tail of a fish is vertical and moves from side to side when the fish swims. The tail of a cetacean—called a fluke—is horizontal and moves up and down, as cetaceans' spines bend in the same manner as a human spine.

Pinniped

Pinnipeds or fin-footed mammals are a widely distributed and diverse group of semi-aquatic marine mammals comprising the families Odobenidae (walruses), Otariidae (eared seals, including sea lions and fur seals), and Phocidae (earless seals). Formerly classified as a separate biological suborder, *Pinnipedia* is now sometimes considered a superfamily within Caniformia, a suborder in the Carnivora order.

Evolution

Recent molecular evidence suggests that pinnipeds evolved from a bearlike ancestor about 23 million years ago during the late Oligocene or early Miocene epochs, a transitional period between the warmer Paleogene and cooler Neogene period The earliest fossil pinniped that has been found is *Enaliarctos,* which lived 24 - 22 million years ago. It is believed to have been a good swimmer, but to have been able to move on land as well as in water, more like an otter than like modern pinnipeds. There has been longstanding debate as to whether walruses diverged from a common otariid-phocid ancestor, or whether the phocids diverged before a common otariid-odobenid ancestor. The most recent evidence suggest that the latter hypothesis is more likely.

Pinnipeds are typically sleek-bodied, barrel-shaped and can be rather large. Their bodies are well adapted to the aquatic habitat where they spend most of their lives. Their limbs have evolved into short, wide, flat flippers whence the name (derived from the Latin *pinna* = "feather", "wing" or "fin", and *ped* = foot). The smallest pinniped, the Galapagos fur seal, weighs about 30 kg (65 lb) when full-grown and is 1.2 m (4 ft) long; the largest, the male southern elephant seal, is over 4 m (13 ft) long andeighsup to 2,200 kg than 2 tons).

Otariidae

Eared seals, also called "walking seals" and "otariids", include the animals commonly known as sea lions and fur seals. These are vocal, social animals that are somewhat better adapted to terrestrial habitats with rear flippers that can turn forward such that they can move on all fours on land. Their foreflippers are larger than those of earless seals and are used as a primary source of maneuverability in the water. Eared seals have external ears, as their name suggests, and more dog-like snouts, further distinguishing them from the true seals. While sea lions are generally larger than fur seals and lack the dense underfur of the latter, the long-standing division into subfamilies (*Arctocephalinae* and *Otariinae* for fur seals and sea lions respectively) has been shown to be unjustified in light of recent genetic evidence suggesting that several fur seal species are more closely related to some sea lions than other fur seals. The iconic ball-balancing circus seal is generally some species of sea lion, most commonly a California sea lion.

Phocidae

Earless seals, also called "true seals" or "phocids" are the most diverse and widespread of the pinnipeds. They lack external ears and more streamlined snouts and are generally more aquatically adapted. They swim with efficient undulating whole body movements using their more developed rear flippers. The efficiency of their swimming and an array of other physiological adaptations make them better built for deep and long diving and long distance migrations. They are, however, very cumbersome on land, moving by wriggling their front flippers and abdominal muscles. True seals generally communicate by slapping the water and grunting, rather than vocalizing.

Odobenidae

The walrus is an exclusively Arctic species - the sole surviving member of the once diverse and widespread *Odobenidae* family. They are easily recognized by their long tusks and great bulk (up to 2000 kg). While they share with otariids the ability to turn their rear flippers forward, their swimming is more reminiscent of that of true seals, relying more on sinuous whole body movements. They also lack external ears. Unlike eared seals and true seals, which feed primarily by hunting fish and squid in the water column, walrus generally prefer benthic invertebrates, in particular clams. It is the development of the unique squirt and suck method of feeding on molluscs that differentiated the original walrus ancestor from the other pinniped lineages. There remains debate as to whether the walrus diverged from the eared seals before or after the true seals.

ADAPTATIONS

Flippers

Pinnipeds have proportionally shorter limbs than most other mammals. As noted above, their limbs have evolved into flippers with true seals having more developed hind flippers and eared seals having more developed fore flippers. The walrus is intermediate between the two. A pinniped's fingers and toes are bound together by a web of skin. They also have claws that are found either on the front flippers (earless seals) or back flippers (eared seals). Because water has a much higher density than air, their flippers can be much smaller proportionately in relation to their size than the wings of a bird or bat. Additionally, pinnipeds are essentially weightless in the water, allowing them to come to a standstill, and perform aquabatic feats in water that would be impossible for atmospheric flying creatures.

Pinnipeds can hold their breath for nearly two hours underwater.

Oxygen Conservation

Pinnipeds can conserve oxygen for long period of time underwater. When the animal starts diving its heart rate slows to about one-tenth of the normal rate. The arteries squeeze shut and the sense organs and nervous system are the only organs to continue to receive a normal flow of blood. Pinnipeds are able to resist more pain and fatigue caused by lactic acid accumulation than other mammals. However, once they return to the water surface, they need time to recover and bring their body chemistry back to normal

Warmth

Please help improve this section by expanding it. Further information might be found on the talk page or at requests for expansion.

To keep warm in cold waters, pinnipeds have a layer of blubber under their skin, providing buoyancy, and caloric energy. Newborn pinnipeds have no blubber.

Molting

Like other mammals, pinnipeds have to shed their fur once in a while. Eared seals shed more slowly than earless seals. Most earless seals spend time in the water while molting.

Other Adaptations

A pinniped's eyes are well adapted for seeing both above and below the water. When diving the animal has a clear membrane that covers and protects its eyes. In addition, its nostrils close automatically. Testicles and mammary glands are located in slits under the skin to keep the pinniped's streamlined shape. They also have whiskers to help navigate and sensors in their skull to absorb sounds underwater and trasmit them to the cochlea.

Feeding

All pinnipeds are carnivorous, eating fish, shellfish, squid, and other marine creatures. Most are generalist feeders, but some are specialists. For example; Ross Seals and Southern elephant seals mainly feed on squid. Crabeater seals eat mostly krill, and Ringed seals feed almost exclusively on crustaceans. Additionally, the Walrus consumes molluscan prey items by sucking the soft.

Some seals will even eat warm-blooded prey including other seals. The leopard seal, which is probably the most carnivorous and predatory of all the pinnipeds, will eat penguins as well as Crabeater and Ross Seals. The South American sea lion also eats penguin as well as flying seabirds and young South American fur seals. Steller sea lions have been recorded eating Northern fur seal pups, Common seal pups and birds.

Almost all pinnipeds are potential prey for orcas and larger sharks. Arctic species are an important component of polar bear diet.

Reproduction

Males of many species, (e.g. elephant seals, South American sea lions and Northern fur seals) aggressively defend groups of specific females, referred to as harems. Males of other species (e.g. most sea lions and Cape fur seals) defend territories on reproductive rookeries while females move freely between them. Some form of competition, either for females or territories, some of which can be violent, is an integral part of the male breeding strategy among most pinnipeds. Otariids, which are generally more land-adapted, tend to form major aggregations in the summer months on beaches or rocky outcrops. Consequently, their reproductive behavior is easier to observe and well studied. Walruses and many phocids, on the other hand, tend to form smaller aggregations, often in remote locations or on ice, and copulate in the water. Their reproductive behavior is therefore generally less well known.

Females have a postpartum oestrus allowing them to mate soon after giving birth. Subsequent implantation of the embryo is delayed (embryonic diapause) thus removing the need to come ashore (haul-out) twice, once to give birth and again later to mate. After giving birth, mothers suckle their young for a variable length of time. Amongst the phocids, lactation varies from 4 to

50 days, whereas the otarids may lactate from 4 to 36 months. This reflects the fact that phocid feeding grounds tend to be a long way off-shore, so lactation is associated with maternal fasting. To compensate for the short lactation period, the fat content of phocid milk is higher than in any other species of marine mammal (45–60% fat). After lactation most female phocids make extensive migratory movements to feeding grounds for intensive foraging to recoup depleted energy reserves. On the other hand, otariid feeding grounds are generally closer to shore and females go on foraging trips. Fat content of otariid milk is lower than that of the phocids, owing to the protracted lactation period (typically 25–50%). Protracted nursing also leads to the formation of social bonds.

SEA OTTER

The sea otter (*Enhydra lutris*) is a marine mammal native to the coasts of the northern and eastern North Pacific Ocean. Adult sea otters typically weigh between 14 and 45 kg (30 to 100 lb), making them the heaviest members of the weasel family, but among the smallest marine mammals. Unlike most marine mammals, the sea otter's primary form of insulation is an exceptionally thick coat of fur, the densest in the animal kingdom. Although it can walk on land, the sea otter is capable of living exclusively in the ocean.

The sea otter inhabits nearshore environments where it can quickly dive to the sea floor to forage. It preys mostly upon marine invertebrates such as sea urchins, various mollusks and crustaceans, and some species of fish. Its foraging and eating habits are noteworthy in several respects. First, its use of rocks to dislodge prey and to open shells makes it one of the few mammal species to use tools. In most of its range, it is a keystone species, controlling sea urchin populations which would otherwise inflict extensive damage to kelp forest ecosystems. Finally, its diet includes prey species that are also valued by humans as food, leading to conflicts between sea otters and fisheries.

Sea otters, whose numbers were once estimated at 150,000–300,000, were hunted extensively for their fur between 1741 and 1911, and the world population fell to 1,000–2,000 individuals in a fraction of their historic range. A subsequent international ban on hunting, conservation efforts, and reintroduction programs into previously populated areas have contributed to numbers rebounding, and the species now occupies about two-thirds of its former range. The recovery of the sea otter is considered an important success in marine conservation, although populations in the Aleutian Islands and California have recently declined or have plateaued at depressed levels. For these reasons (as well as its particular vulnerability to oil spills) the sea otter remains classified as an endangered species.

The first scientific description of the sea otter is contained in the field notes of Georg Steller from 1751, and the species was described by Linnaeus in his *Systema Naturae* of 1758. Originally named *Lutra marina,* it underwent numerous name changes before being accepted as *Enhydra lutris* in 1922 The generic name *Enhydra,* the Latin word *lutris,* meaning "otter". It was formerly sometimes referred to as the "sea beaver" although it is only distantly related to beavers. It is not to be confused with the marine otter, a rare otter species native to the southern west coast of South America. A number of other otter species, while predominantly living in fresh water, are commonly found in marine coastal habitats as well.

Evolution

Although it is a relatively new marine mammal lineage, the sea otter can live in the ocean at all stages of life.

The sea otter is the heaviest member of the family Mustelidae, a diverse group that includes the thirteen otter species and terrestrial animals such as weasels, badgers, and minks. It is unique among the mustelids in not making dens or burrows, in having no functional anal scent glands, nd in being able to live its entire life without leaving the water The only member of the genus *Enhydra,* the sea otter is so different from other mustelid species that as recently as 1982, some scientists believed it was more closely related to the earless seals. Genetic analysis indicates that the sea otter and its closest extant relatives, which include the African speckle-throated otter, Eurasian otter, African clawless otter and oriental small-clawed otter, shared an ancestor approximately 5 million years ago.

Fossil evidence indicates that the *Enhydra* lineage became isolated in the North Pacific approximately 2 mya, giving rise to the now-extinct *Enhydra macrodonta* and the modern sea otter, *Enhydra lutris* The sea otter evolved initially in northern Hokkaido and Russia, then spread east to the Aleutian Islands, mainland Alaska, and down the North American coast In comparison to cetaceans, sirenians, and pinnipeds, which entered the water approximately 50 mya, 40 mya, and 20 mya, respectively, the sea otter is a relative newcomer to a marine existence. In some respects, however, the sea otter is more fully aquatically adapted than pinnipeds, which must haul out on land or ice to give birth.

Subspecies

There are three recognized subspecies, which vary in body size and in some skull and dental characteristics:

- The common sea otter, *E. l. lutris* ranges from the Kuril Islands to the Commander Islands in the western Pacific Ocean. Also known as the Asian sea otter, it is the largest subspecies with a wide skull and short nasal bones.
- The southern sea otter, *E. l. nereis* (Merriam, 1904), is found off the coast of central California. Also known as the Californian sea otter, it has a narrower skull with a long rostrum and small teeth.
- The northern sea otter, *E. l. kenyoni* (Wilson, 1991), also known as the Alaskan sea otter, is native to the Aleutian Islands and mainland Alaska, but has since been re-introduced to various locations from Alaska to Oregon. While intermediate between the other subspecies in most characteristics, it has longer mandible bones.

Physical Characteristics

The sea otter is one of the smallest marine mammal species. Male sea otters weigh 22 to 45 kg (49 to 99 lb) and are 1.2 to 1.5 m (4 to 5 ft) in length. Females are smaller, weighing 14 to 33 kg (30 to 73 lb) and measuring 1.0 to 1.4 m (3 ft 3 in to 4 ft 7 in) in length.

Unlike other marine mammals, the sea otter has no blubber and relies on its exceptionally thick fur to keep warm With up to 150 thousand strands of hair per square centimeter (nearly one million per sq in), its fur is the most dense of any animal. The fur consists of long waterproof guard hairs and short underfur; the guard hairs keep the dense underfur layer dry. Cold water is thus kept completely away from the skin and heat loss is limited. The fur is thick year-round, as it is shed and replaced gradually rather than in a distinct molting season. As the ability of the guard hairs to repel water depends on utmost cleanliness, the sea otter has the ability to reach and groom the fur on any part of its body, taking advantage of its loose skin and an unusually supple skeleton. The coloration of the pelage is usually deep brown with sliver-gray speckles, however it can range from yellowish or grayish brown to almost black In adults, the head, throat, and chest are lighter in color than the rest of the body.

The sea otter displays numerous adaptations to its marine environment. The nostrils and small ears can close The hind feet, which provide most of its propulsion in swimming, are long, broadly flattened, and fully webbed. The fifth digit on each hind foot is longest, facilitating swimming while on its back, but making walking difficult The tail is fairly short, thick, slightly flattened, and muscular. The front paws are short with retractable claws, with tough pads on the palms that enable gripping slippery prey.

Skeleton of a sea otter. The hind flippers are larger than the mitten-like front paws.

The sea otter propels itself underwater by moving the rear end of its body, including its tail and hind feet, up and down, and is capable of speeds of up to 9 km/h (5.6 mph) When underwater, its body is long and streamlined, with the short forelimbs pressed closely against the chest. When at the surface, it usually floats on its back and moves by sculling its feet and tail from side to side. At rest, all four limbs can be folded onto the torso to conserve heat, whereas on particularly hot days the hind feet may be held underwater for cooling. The sea otter's body is highly buoyant because of its large lung capacity – about 2.5 times greater than that of similarly-sized land mammals - and the air trapped in its fur. The sea otter walks with a clumsy rolling gait on land, and can run in a bounding motion.

Long, highly sensitive whiskers and front paws help the sea otter find prey by touch when waters are dark or murky Researchers have noted that when they approach in plain view, sea otters react more rapidly when the wind is blowing towards the animals, indicating that the sense of smell is more important than sight as a warning sense. Other observations indicate that the sea otter's sense of sight is useful above and below the water, although not as good as that of seals. Its hearing is neither particularly acute nor poor.

An adult's 32 teeth, particularly the molars, are flattened and rounded, designed to crush rather than cut food Seals and sea otters are the only carnivores with two pairs of lower incisor teeth rather than three.

The sea otter has a metabolic rate two or three times that of comparatively sized terrestrial mammals. It must eat an estimated 25 to 38% of its own body weight in food each day in order to burn the calories necessary to counteract the loss of heat due to the cold water environment. Its digestive efficiency is estimated at 80 to 85%, and food is digested and passed in as little as three hours. Most of its need for water is met through food, although, in contrast to most other marine mammals, it also drinks seawater. Its relatively large kidneys enable it to derive fresh water from sea water and excrete concentrated urine.

Behaviour

Sensitive whiskers and forepaws enable sea otters to find prey using their sense of touch.

The sea otter is diurnal. It has a period of foraging and eating in the morning, starting about an hour before sunrise, then rests or sleeps in mid-day. Foraging resumes for a few hours in the afternoon and subsides before sunset, and there may be a third foraging period around midnight. Females with pups appear to be more inclined to feed at night. Observations of the amount of time a sea otter must spend each day foraging range from 24 to

60%, apparently depending on the availability of food in the area.

The sea otter spends much of its time grooming, which consists of cleaning the fur, untangling knots, removing loose fur, rubbing the fur to squeeze out water and introduce air, and blowing air into the fur. To an observer it appears as if the animal is scratching, however sea otters are not known to have lice or other parasites in the fur. When eating, the sea otter rolls in the water frequently, apparently to wash food scraps from its fur.

The sea otter hunts in short dives, often to the sea floor. Although it can hold its breath for up to five minutes dives typically last about one minute and no more than four It is the only marine animal capable of lifting and turning over boulders, which it often does with its front paws when searching for prey The sea otter may also pluck snails and other organisms from kelp and dig deep into underwater mud for clams It is the only marine mammal that catches fish with its forepaws rather than with its teeth.

Under each foreleg, the sea otter has a loose pouch of skin that extends across the chest. In this pouch (preferentially the left one), the animal stores collected food to bring to the surface. here, the sea otter eats while floating on its back, using its forepaws to tear food apart and bring it to its mouth. It can chew and swallow small mussels with their shells, whereas large mussel shells may be twisted apart It uses its lower incisor teeth to access the meat in shellfish. To eat large sea urchins, which are mostly covered with spines, the sea otter bites through the underside where the spines are shortest, and licks the soft contents out of the urchin's shell.

The sea otter's use of rocks when hunting and feeding makes it one of the few mammal species to use tools To open hard shells, it may pound its prey with both paws against a rock on its chest. To pry an abalone off its rock, it hammers the abalone shell using a large stone, with observed rates of 45 blows in 15 seconds. Releasing an abalone, which can cling to rock with a force equal to 4,000 times its own body weight, requires multiple dives.

Although each adult and independent juvenile forages alone, sea otters tend to rest together in single-sex groups called *rafts.* A raft typically contains 10 to 100 animals, with male rafts being larger than female ones The largest raft ever seen contained over 2000 sea otters. To keep from drifting out to sea when resting and eating, sea otters may wrap themselves in kelp.

A male sea otter is most likely to mate if he maintains a breeding territory in an area that is also favored by females As autumn is the peak breeding season in most areas, males typically defend their territory only from spring to autumn. During this time, males patrol the boundaries of their territories to exclude other males lthough actual fighting is rare Adult females move freely between male territories, where they outnumber adult males by an average of five to one. Males who do not have territories tend to congregate in large male-only groups and swim through female areas when searching for a mate.

The species exhibits a variety of vocal behaviors. The cry of a pup is often compared to that of a seagull Females coo when they are apparently content; males may grunt instead Distressed or frightened adults may whistle, hiss, or in extreme circumstances, scream. Although sea otters can be playful and sociable, they are not considered to be truly social animals hey spend much time alone, and each adult can meet its own needs in terms of hunting, grooming, and defense.

Reproduction and Lifecycle

During mating, the male bites the nose of the female, often bloodying and scarring it.

Sea otters are polygynous: males have multiple female partners. However, temporary pair-bonding occurs for a few days between a female in estrus and her mate. Mating takes place in the water and can be rough, the male biting the female on the muzzle - which often leaves scars on the nose - and sometimes holding her head under water.

Births occur year-round, with peaks between May and June in northern populations and between January and March in southern populations Gestation appears to vary from four to twelve months, as the species is capable of delayed implantation followed by four months of pregnancy. In California, sea otters usually breed every year, about twice as often as sea otters in Alaska. ace in the water and typically produces a single pup weighing 1.4 to 2.3 kg Twins occur in 2% of births; however, usually only one pup survives. At birth, the eyes are open, ten teeth are visible, and the pup has a thick coat of baby fur Mothers have been observed to lick and fluff a newborn for hours; after grooming, the pup's fur retains so much air that the pup floats like a cork and cannot dive The fluffy baby fur is replaced by adult fur after about thirteen weeks.

Nursing lasts six to eight months in California populations and four to twelve months in Alaska, with the mother beginning to offer bits of prey at one to two months The milk from a sea otter's two abdominal nipples is rich in fat and more similar to the milk of other marine mammals than to that of other mustelids A pup, with guidance from its mother, practices swimming and diving for several weeks before it is able to reach the sea floor. Initially the objects it retrieves are of little food value, such as brightly colored starfish and pebbles. Juveniles are typically independent at six to eight months, however a mother may be forced to abandon a pup if she cannot find enough food for it and at the other extreme, a pup may nurse until it is almost adult size Pup mortality is high, particularly during an individual's first winter - by one estimate, only 25% of pups survive their first year. Pups born to experienced mothers have the highest survival rates.

Females perform all tasks of feeding and raising offspring, and have occasionally been observed caring for orphaned pups. Much has been written about the level of devotion of sea otter mothers for their pups - a mother gives her infant almost constant attention, cradling it on her chest away from the cold water and attentively grooming its fur. When foraging, she leaves her pup floating on the water, sometimes wrapped in kelp to keep it from floating away if the pup is not sleeping, it cries loudly until she returns Mothers have been known to carry their pup for days after the pup's deat.

Females become sexually mature at around three or four years of age and males at around five; however, males often do not successfully breed until a few years later. A captive male sired offspring at age 19. In the wild, sea otters live to a maximum age of 23 years, with average lifespans of 10–15 years for males and 15–20 years for females Several captive individuals have lived past 20 years, and a female at the Seattle Aquarium died at the age of 28 years. Sea otters in the wild often develop worn teeth, which may account for their apparently shorter lifespans.

Population and Distribution

Sea otters live in coastal waters 15 to 23 meters (50 to 75 ft) deep, and usually stay within a kilometre of the shore. They are found most often in areas with protection from the most severe ocean winds, such as rocky coastlines, thick kelp forests, and barrier reefs Although they are most strongly associated with rocky substrates, sea otters can also live in areas where the sea floor consists primarily of mud, sand, or silt. Their northern range is limited by ice, as sea otters can survive amidst drift ice but not land-fast ice Individuals generally occupy a home range a few kilometers long, and remain there year-round.

The sea otter population is thought to have once been 150,000 to 300,000 stretching in an arc across the North Pacific from northern Japan to the central Baja Peninsula in Mexico. The fur trade that began in the 1740s reduced the sea otter's numbers to an estimated 1000 to 2000 members in thirteen colonies. In about two-thirds of its former range, the species is at varying levels of recovery, with high population densities in some areas and threatened populations in others. Sea otters currently have stable populations in parts of the Russian east coast, Alaska, British Columbia, Washington, and California, and there have been reports of recolonizations in Mexico and Japan. Population estimates made between 2004 and 2007 give a worldwide total of approximately 107,000 sea otters.

Russia

Currently, the most stable and secure part of the sea otter's range is Russia. Before the 19th century there were around 20,000 to 25,000 sea otters in the Kuril Islands, with more on Kamchatka and the Commander Islands. After the years of the Great Hunt, the population in these areas, currently part of Russia, was only 750. As of 2004, sea otters have repopulated all of their former habitat in these areas, with an estimated total population of about 27,000. Of these, about 19,000 are in the Kurils, 2000 to 3500 on Kamchatka and another 5000 to 5500 on the Commander Islands. Growth has slowed slightly, suggesting that the numbers are reaching carrying capacity.

Alaska

Alaska is the heartland of the sea otter's range. In 1973, the sea otter population in Alaska was estimated at between 100,000 and 125,000 animals. By 2006, however, the Alaska population had fallen to an estimated 73,000 animals A massive decline in sea otter populations in the Aleutian Islands accounts for most of the change; the cause of this decline is not known, although orca predation is suspected. The sea otter population in Prince William Sound was also hit hard by the Exxon Valdez oil spill, which killed thousands of sea otters in 1989.

British Columbia and Washington

Along the North American coast south of Alaska, the sea otter's range is discontinuous. Between 1969 and 1972, 89 sea otters were flown or shipped from Alaska to the west coast of Vancouver Island, British Columbia. They established a healthy population, estimated to be over 3,000 as of 2004, and their range is now from Tofino to Cape Scott In 1989, a separate colony was discovered in the central British Columbia coast. It is not known if this colony, which had a size of about 300 animals in 2004, was founded by transplanted otters or by survivors of the fur trade.

In 1969 and 1970, 59 sea otters were translocated from Amchitka Island to Washington. Annual surveys between 2000 and 2004 have recorded between 504 and 743 individuals, and their range is in the Olympic Peninsula from just south of Destruction Island to Pillar Point.

In British Columbia and Washington, sea otters are found almost exclusively on the outer coasts. Reported sightings of sea otters in the San Juan Islands and Puget Sound almost always turn out to be northern river otters which are commonly seen along the seashore. However, biologists have confirmed isolated sightings of sea otters in these areas since the mid-1990s.

California

The spring 2007 sea otter survey counted 3,026 sea otters in the central California coast, down from an estimated pre-fur trade population of 16,000. California's sea otters are the descendants of a single colony of about 50 southern sea otters discovered near Big Sur in 1938; their principal range is now from just south of San Francisco to Santa Barbara County. In the late 1980s, the U.S. Fish and Wildlife Service relocated about 140 California sea otters to San Nicolas Island in southern California, in the hope of establishing a reserve population should the mainland be struck by an oil spill. To the surprise of biologists, the San Nicholas population initially shrank as the animals migrated back to the mainland, As of 2005, only 30 sea otters remained at San Nicholas, thriving on the abundant prey around the island. The plan that authorized the translocation program had predicted that carrying capacity would be reached within 5 to 10 years.

When the Fish and Wildlife Service implemented the translocation programme, it also attempted to implement "zonal management" of the California population. To manage the competition between sea otters and fisheries, it declared an "otter-free zone" stretching from Point Conception to the Mexican border. In this zone, only San Nicolas Island was designated as sea otter habitat, and sea otters found elsewhere in the area were supposed to be captured and relocated. These plans were abandoned after it proved impractical to capture the hundreds of otters which ignored regulations and swam into the zone. However, after engaging in a period of public commentary in 2005, the Fish and Wildlife Service has yet to release a formal decision on the issue.

Ecology

Sea otters keep kelp forests healthy by eating animals that graze on kelp.

Sea otters consume over 100 different prey species. In most of its range, the sea otter's diet consists almost exclusively of marine invertebrates, including sea urchins, a variety of bivalves such as clams and mussels, abalone, other mollusks, crustaceans, and snails. ts prey ranges in size from tiny limpets crabs to giant octopuses Where prey such as sea urchins, clams, and abalone are present in a range of sizes, sea otters tend to select larger items over smaller ones of similar type In California, it has been noted that sea otters ignore Pismo clams smaller than 3 inches (7 cm) across.

In a few northern areas, fish are also eaten. In studies performed at Amchitka Island in the 1960s, where the sea otter population was at carrying capacity, 50% of food found in sea otter stomachs was fish The fish species were usually bottom-dwelling and sedentary or sluggish forms, such as the red Irish lord and globefish However, south of Alaska on the North American coast, fish are a negligible or extremely minor part of the sea otter's diet. Contrary to popular depictions, sea otters rarely eat starfish, and any kelp that is consumed apparently passes through the sea otter's system undigested

The individuals within a particular area often differ in their foraging methods and their prey types, and tend to follow the same patterns as their mothers The diet of local populations also changes over time, as sea otters can significantly deplete populations of highly preferred prey such as large sea urchins, and prey availability is also affected by other factors such as fishing by humans Sea otters can thoroughly remove abalone from an area except for specimens in deep rock crevices, however, they never completely wipe out a prey species from an area. A study demonstrated that in areas where food was relatively scarce, a wider variety of prey was consumed. However, surprisingly, the diets of individuals were more specialized in these areas than in areas where food was plentiful.

As a Keystone Species

Sea otters are a classic example of a keystone species; their presence affects the ecosystem more profoundly than their size and numbers would suggest. Sea otters keep the population of certain benthic (sea floor) herbivores, particularly sea urchins, in check. Sea urchins graze on the lower stems of kelp, causing the kelp to drift away and die. Loss of the habitat and nutrients provided by kelp forests leads to profound cascade effects on the marine ecosystem. North Pacific areas that do not have sea otters often turn into urchin barrens, with abundant sea urchins and no kelp forest.

Remote areas of coastline, such as this area in California, sheltered the few remaining colonies of sea otters that survived the fur trade.

Reintroduction of sea otters to British Columbia has led to a dramatic improvement in the health of coastal ecosystems and similar changes have been observed as sea otter populations recovered in the Aleutian and Commander Islands and the Big Sur coast of California However, some kelp forest ecosystems in California have also thrived without sea otters, with sea urchin populations apparently controlled by other factors. The role of sea otters in maintaining kelp forests has been observed to be more important in areas of open coast than in more protected bays and estuaries.

In addition to promoting growth of kelp forests, sea otters can also have a profound effect in rocky areas that tend to be dominated by mussel beds. They remove mussels from rocks, liberating space for competitive species and thereby increasing the diversity of species in the area.

Predators

Predators of sea otters include orcas and sea lions; bald eagles also prey on pups by snatching them from the water surface. In California, bites from sharks, particularly great white sharks, have been estimated to cause 10% of sea otter deaths and are one of the reasons the population has not expanded further north Dead sea otters have been found with injuries from shark bites.

Relationship with Humans

Archaeological evidence indicates that for thousands of years, indigenous peoples have hunted sea otters in moderation for food and fur. Large-scale hunting, which would eventually kill approximately one million sea otters, began in the 1700s when hunters and traders began to arrive from all over the world to meet foreign demand for otter pelts, which were one of the world's most valuable types of fur.

In the early 1700s, Russians began to hunt sea otters in the Kuril Islands and sold them to China Russia was also exploring the far northern Pacific at this time, and sent Vitus Bering to map the Arctic coast and find routes from Siberia to North America In 1741, on his second North Pacific voyage, Bering was shipwrecked off Bering Island in the Commander Islands, where Bering and many of his crew died. The surviving crew members, which included naturalist Georg Steller, discovered sea otters on the beaches of the island and spent the winter hunting sea otters and gambling with otter pelts. They returned to Siberia having killed nearly 1000 sea otters, and were able to command high prices for the pelts Thus began what is sometimes called the "Great Hunt", which would continue for another hundred years.

Russian fur-hunting expeditions soon depleted the sea otter populations in the Commander Islands, and by 1745 they began to move on to the Aleutian Islands. The Russians initially traded with the Aleuts inhabitants of these islands for otter pelts, but later enslaved the Aleuts, taking women and children hostage and torturing and killing Aleut men to force them to hunt. Many Aleuts were either murdered by the Russians or died from diseases that the hunters had introduced. The Aleut population was reduced, by the Russians' own estimate, from 20000 to 2000. By the 1760s, the Russians had reached Alaska. Other nations joined in the hunt in the south. Along the coasts of what is now Mexico and California, Spanish explorers bought sea otter pelts from Native Americans and sold them in Asia In 1778, British explorer Captain James Cook reached Vancouver Island and bought sea otter furs from the First Nations people. When Cook's ship later stopped at a Chinese port, the pelts rapidly sold at high prices, and were soon known as "soft gold". As word spread, people from all over Europe and North America began to arrive in the Pacific Northwest to trade for sea otter furs.

Russian hunting expanded to the south, in what is now Washington, Oregon, and California, and the Russians founded what is now the Fort Ross settlement in northern California as their southern headquarters. In the next 29 years, they would kill 50,000 California sea otters.

Eventually, sea otter populations became so depleted that commercial hunting was no longer viable. In the Aleutian Islands, commercial hunting had stopped by 1808 When Russia sold Alaska to the United States in 1867, the Alaska population had recovered to over 100,000, but Americans resumed hunting and quickly extirpated the sea otter again Prices rose as the species became rare. During the 1880s, a pelt brought $105 to $165 in the London market, however by 1903 a pelt could be worth as much as $1,125. In 1911, Russia, Japan, Great Britain (for Canada) and the United States signed the Treaty for the Preservation and Protection of Fur Seals, imposing a moratorium on the harvesting of sea otters. So few remained, perhaps only 1,000–2,000 individuals in the wild, that many believed the species would become extinct.

During the 20th century, sea otter numbers rebounded in about two-thirds of their historic range, a recovery that is considered one of the greatest successes in marine conservation However, the IUCN lists the sea otter as an endangered species, and describes the significant threats to sea otters as oil pollution, predation by orcas, poaching, and conflicts with fisheries – sea otters can drown if entangled in fishing gear. The hunting of sea otters is no longer legal except for limited harvests by indigenous peoples in the United States. Poaching was a serious concern in the Russian Far East immediately after the collapse of the Soviet Union in 1991, however it has declined significantly with stricter law enforcement and better economic conditions.

The most significant threat to sea otters is oil spills. Sea otters are particularly vulnerable, as they rely on their fur to keep warm. When their fur is soaked with oil, it loses its ability to retain air, and the animal quickly dies from hypothermia The liver, kidneys, and lungs of sea otters also become damaged after they inhale oil or ingest it when grooming. The Exxon Valdez oil spill of

24 March 1989 killed thousands of sea otters in Prince William Sound, and as of 2006 the lingering oil in the area continues to affect the population. Describing the public sympathy for sea otters that developed from media coverage of the event, a U.S. Fish and Wildlife Service spokesperson wrote:

> As a playful, photogenic, innocent bystander, the sea otter epitomized the role of victim . . . cute and frolicsome sea otters suddenly in distress, oiled, frightened, and dying, in a losing battle with the oil.

The small geographic ranges of the sea otter populations in California, Washington, and British Columbia mean that a single major spill could be catastrophic for that state or province Prevention of oil spills and preparation for the rescue of otters in the event of one are major areas of focus for conservation efforts. Increasing the size and the range of sea otter populations would also reduce the risk of an oil spill wiping out a population However, because of the species' reputation for depleting shellfish resources, advocates for commercial, recreational, and subsistence shellfish harvesting have often opposed allowing the sea otter's range to increase, and there have even been instances of fishermen and others illegally killing them.

In the Aleutian Islands, a massive and unexpected disappearance of sea otters has occurred in recent decades. In the 1980s, the area was home to an estimated 55,000 to 100,000 sea otters, but the population fell to around 6000 animals by 2000. The most widely-accepted, but still controversial, hypothesis is that orcas have been eating the otters. The pattern of sea otter disappearances is consistent with a rise in orca predation, however there has been no direct evidence that orcas prey on sea otters to any significant extent.

Another area of concern is California, where recovery began to fluctuate or decline in the late 1990s. Unusually high mortality rates amongst adult and sub-adult otters, particularly females, have been reported Necropsies of dead sea otters indicate that diseases, particularly *Toxoplasma gondii* infection and acanthocephalan parasite infection, are a major cause of sea otter mortality in California. The *Toxoplasma gondii* parasite, which is often fatal to sea otters, is carried by wild and domestic cats and by opossums, and may be transmitted by domestic cat droppings flushed into the ocean via the sewage system Although it is clear that disease has contributed to the deaths of many of California's sea otters, it is not known why the California population is apparently more affected by disease than populations in other areas.

Sea otter habitat is preserved through several protected areas in the United States, Russia and Canada. In marine protected areas, polluting activities such as dumping of waste and oil drilling are typically prohibited. There are estimated to be more than 1,200 sea otters within the Monterey Bay National Marine Sanctuary, and more than 500 within the Olympic Coast National Marine Sanctuary.

Economic Impact

Some of the sea otter's preferred prey species, particularly abalone, clams, and crabs, are also food sources for humans. In some areas, massive declines in shellfish harvests have been blamed on the sea otter, and intense public debate has taken place over how to manage the competition between sea otters and humans for seafood.

The debate is complicated by the fact that sea otters have sometimes been held responsible for declines of shellfish stocks that were more likely caused by overfishing by humans, disease, pollution, and seismic activity Shellfish declines have also occurred in many parts of the North American Pacific coast that do not have sea otters, and conservationists sometimes note that the existence of large concentrations of shellfish on the coast is a recent development resulting from the fur trade's near-extirpation of the sea otter Although many factors affect shellfish stocks, sea otter predation can deplete a fishery to the point that it is no longer commercially viable There is a consensus among scientists that sea otters and abalone fisheries cannot co-exist in the same area and the same is likely true for certain other types of shellfish as well.

There are many facets to the interaction between sea otters and the human economy that are not as immediately felt. Sea otters have been credited with contributing to the kelp harvesting industry via their well-known role in controlling sea urchin populations; kelp is used in the production of diverse food and pharmaceutical products. Although human divers harvest red sea urchins both for food and to protect the kelp, sea otters hunt more sea urchin species and are more consistently effective in controlling these populations The health of the kelp forest ecosystem is significant in nurturing populations of fish, including commercially important fish species In some areas, sea otters are a popular tourist attraction, bringing visitors to local hotels, restaurants, and sea otter-watching expeditions.

Role in Human Cultures

For many maritime indigenous cultures throughout the North Pacific, especially the Ainu in the Kuril Islands, the Koryaks and Itelmen of Kamchatka, the Aleut in the Aleutian Islands and a host of tribes on the Pacific coast of North America, the sea otter has played an important role as a cultural as well as material resource. In these cultures, many of which have strongly animist traditions full of legends and stories in which many aspects of the natural world are associated with spirits, the sea otter was considered particularly kin to humans. The Nuu-chah-nulth, Haida, and other First Nations of coastal British Columbia used the warm and luxurious pelts as chiefs' regalia. Sea otter pelts were given in potlatches to mark coming-of-age ceremonies, weddings, and funerals The Aleuts carved sea otter bones for use as ornaments and in games, and used powdered sea otter baculum as a medicine for fever.

Among the Ainu, the otter is portrayed as an occasional messenger between humans and the creator. Versions of a widespread Aleut legend tell of lovers or despairing women who plunge into the sea and become otters These links have been associated with the many human-like behavioral features of the sea otter, including apparent playfulness, strong mother-pup bonds and tool use, yielding to ready anthropomorphism. The beginning of commercial exploitation had a great impact on the human as well as animal populations – the Ainu and Aleuts have been displaced or their numbers are dwindling, while the coastal tribes of North America, where the otter is in any case greatly depleted, no longer rely as intimately on sea mammals for survival.

Since the mid-1970s, the beauty and charisma of the species have gained wide appreciation, and the sea otter has become an icon of environmental conservation. The round, expressive face and soft furry body of the sea otter are depicted in a wide variety of souvenirs, postcards, clothing, and stuffed toys.

12

Bacteriopages

Introduction

A bacteriophage (from 'bacteria' and Greek *phagein*, 'to eat') is a virus that infects bacteria. The term is commonly used in its shortened form, phage. Like viruses that infect eukaryotes (plants, animals and fungi), a large diversity of phage structures and functions exist. Typically, they consist of an outer protein hull enclosing genetic material. The genetic material can be either RNA or DNA, but is usually double-stranded DNA between 5 and 500 kilo base pairs long. Bacteriophages are usually between 20 and 200 nm in size.

Phages are ubiquitous and can be found in many reservoirs populated by bacteria, such as soil or the intestine of animals. One of the densest natural sources for phages and other viruses is sea water, where up to 109 virions per millilitre have been found at the surface, and up to 70% of marine bacteria may be infected by phages.

In 1915, British bacteriologist Frederick Twort discovered a small agent that infects and kills bacteria, but did not pursue the issue further. Independently, French-Canadian microbiologist Félix d'Hérelle announced on 3rd September, 1917 that he discovered "an invisible, antagonistic microbe of the dysentery bacillus" which he named bacteriophage.

Various other phage morphologies have been observed, such as the long, filamentous Inoviridae family, rod-like structures, or the spherical Cystoviridae family.

Replication

Bacteriophages may have a lytic cycle or a lysogenic cycle, however a few viruses are capable of carrying out both. In the lytic cycle, characteristic of virulent phages such as the T4 phage, host cells will be broken open (lysed) and suffer death after immediate replication of the virion. As soon as the cell is destroyed the viruses will have to find new hosts.

In contrast, the lysogenic cycle does not result in immediate lysing of the host cell, those phages able to undergo lysogeny are known s temperate phages. Their viral genome will integrate with host DNA and replicate along with it fairly harmlessly, or may even become established as a plasmid. The virus remains dormant until host conditions deteriorate, perhaps due to depletion of nutrients, then the endogenous phages (known as prophages) become active. They initiate the reproductive cycle resulting in the lysis of the host cell. Interestingly, as the lysogenic cycle allows the host cell to continue to survive and reproduce the virus is reproduced in all of the cell's offspring.

Sometime prophages may provide benefits to the host bacterium whil they are dormant by adding new functions to the bacterial genome in a phenomenon called lysogenic conversion. A famous example is the conversion of a harmless strain of *Vibrio cholerae* by a phage into a highly virulent one, which causes cholera.

Attachment and Penetration

To enter a host cell, bacteriophages attach to specific receptors on the surface of bacteria, including lipopolysaccharides, teichoic acids, proteins or even flagella. This specificity means that a bacteriophage can only infect certain bacteria bearing receptors that they can bind to. As phage virions do not move, they must rely on random encounters with the right receptors when in solution (blood and lymphatic circulation).

Complex bacteriophages, such as the T-even phages, are thought to use a syringe-like motion to inject their genetic material into the cell. After making contact with the appropriate receptor, the tail fibres bring the base plate closer to the surface of the cell. Once attached completely, conformational changes cause the tail to contract, possibly with the help of ATP present in the tail. While the genetic material may be pushed through the membrane, it can also be deposited on the cell surface. Other bacteriophages may use different methods to insert their genetic material.

Synthesis of Proteins and Nucleic Acid

Within a short amount of time, sometimes just minutes, bacterial ribosomes start translating viral mRNA into protein. For RNA-based phages, RNA replicase is synthesised early in the process. Early proteins and a few proteins that were present in the virion may modify the bacterial RNA polymerase so that it preferentially transcribes viral mRNA. The host's normal synthesis of proteins and nucleic acids is disrupted, and it is forced to manufacture viral products. These products go on to become part of new virions within the cell, helper proteins which help assemble the new virions, or proteins involved in cell lysis.

Virion Assembly

In the case of the T4 phage, the construction of new virus particles is a complex process which requires the assistance of special helper molecules. The base plate is assembled first, with the tail being built upon it afterwards. The head capsid, constructed separately, will spontaneously assemble with the tail. The DNA is packed efficiently within the head in a manner which is not yet known. The whole process takes about 15 minutes.

Release of Virions

Phages may be released via cell lysis or by host cell secretion. In the case of the T4 phage, in just over twenty minutes after injection upwards of three hundred phages will be released via lysis. This is achieved by an enzyme called endolysin which attacks and breaks down the peptidoglycan. Some phages however may become long-term [parasite]s and make the host cell continually secrete new virus particles. The new virions bud off the plasma membrane, taking a portion of it with them to become enveloped viruses possessing a viral envelope. All released virions are capable of infecting a new bacterium.

A 3D render of a T4 type bacteriophage landing on a bacterium to inject genetic materialPhages were tried as anti-bacterial agents after their discovery. However Antibiotics, upon their discovery, proved to be more practical. Research on phage therapy was largely discontinued in the West, but phage therapy has been used since the 1940s in the former Soviet Union as an alternative to antibiotics for treating bacterial infections.

The Evolution of Bacterial Strains

The evolution of bacterial strains through natural selection that are resistant to multiple drugs has led some medical researchers to re-evaluate phages as alternatives to the use of antibiotics. Unlike antibiotics, phages adapt along with the bacteria, as they have done for millions of years, so a sustained resistance is unlikely. Additionally, when an effective phage has been found it will seek out the bacteria and continue to kill bacteria of that type until they are all gone.

A specific type of phage often infects only one specific type of bacterium (ranging from several species, to only certain subtypes within a species), so one has to make sure to identify the correct type of bacteria, which takes about 24 hours. An added advantage is that no other bacteria are attacked, making it work similarly to a narrow spectrum antibiotic. However this is a disadvantage in infections with several different types of bacteria, which is often the case. Sometimes mixes of several strains of phage are used to create a broader spectrum cure. Another problem with bacteriophages is that they are attacked by the body's immune system.

Phages work best when in direct contact with the infection, so they are best applied directly to an open wound. This is rarely applicable in the current clinical setting where infections occur systemically. Despite individual success in the former USSR where other therapies had failed, many researchers studying infectious diseases question whether phage therapy will achieve any medical relevance. There have been no large clinical trials to test the efficacy of phage therapy yet, but research continues because of the rise of multiple antibiotic resistance.

13

Cultivation of Marine Sponges

Introduction

The seas and oceans occupy approximately 70% of the earth surface The inaccessibility of these waters to humans for many centuries resulted in much speculation about fantastic animals that would inhabit the deep oceans The development of submarines, scuba diving and under water cameras revealed that indeed peculiar animals were present at the sea floors, for example sponges Sponges are the most simple and ancient multicellular animals on earth and live attached to the seabed or another substratum. They show a circumpolar distribution and inhabit all seas from Greece to Antarctic and from Indonesia to Norway and from great depths (where they are exposed to high pressure) to coastal waters (Some species may reach a height of more than two meters, whereas others are tiny encrusting species with diameters of no more than a few centimetres . The huge diversity with respect to their natural habitat is probably the reason for the estimated number of approximately 15,000 different sponge species (Hooper et al., 2002).

In the introduction of this thesis it is described what sponges do to support life, their general biology and why mankind is interested in sponges. In the last part of the introduction the aim of this thesis is outlined.

Mode of Action

To support life, sponges pump huge amounts of seawater (170-72,000 × their own body volume per day) through their bodies and filtrate it to capture food particles, such as bacteria, micro algae, other unicellular organisms or dead organic particles. The whole sponge body is designed for efficient filtration of the surrounding seawater which is essential because of the low nutrient availability at the sea floor. Water is pumped into the sponge via many small canals that start at the outer surface of the sponge. The water current into the sponge is generated by specialised flagellated cells, called choanocytes, which are clustered in choanocyte chambers in the interior of the sponge. The feeding structures have evolved from originally respiratory structures, but their pumping capacity had to increase many-fold to provide the sponge with a sufficient amount of food. Dissolved oxygen is taken up via inefficient diffusion inside the canals and choanocyte chambers. A more ingenious trap is required to retain nutrients in the processed seawater as their concentration is very low. Choanocytes are sponge cells that are equipped with a collar of microvilli that surrounds the flagellum to withdraw small food particles from the passing seawater. The food particles are stored in food vacuoles of the choanocytes and are passed on to archeocytes. It is generally assumed that archeocytes distribute the nutrients over the rest of the sponge, as they can travel through the sponge.

In addition, there are many other ways for ingestion of food particles. Especially larger particles are taken up directly by archeocytes from the canals before they reach the choanocyte chambers Furthermore, food particles can be taken up by exo- and endopinacocytes that cover the outside of the sponge and the canals and the surfaces inside the sponge Moreover, it has been suggested that sponges are capable of absorbing dissolved organic nutrient directly from the water.

Sponge Bauplan

Skeleton and Mesohyl

Sponges are currently divided into three different classes (hexactinellida, calcarea and demospongiae) based on the nature of their skeleton Calcareous sponges possess a skeleton that is composed entirely of calcite spicules while the hexactinellida, which are primarily deep-water sponges, have a skeleton that is built of six-rayed (hexactinal) siliceous spicules Demospongiae form the largest class, comprising approximately 95% of all species, of which the skeleton is composed of siliceous spicules that is The spicules and collagen fibres form a strong network in the mesohyl that comprises the space between the exopinacoderm and the endopinacoderm. In addition to collagen fibres the mesohyl comprises galectins, fibronectin-like molecules, dermatopontin and polysaccharides These macromolecules form the extracellular matrix, which provides the platform for specific cell adhesion as well as for signal transduction and cell growth. Because of these functions the extracellular matrix plays vital roles in digestion, gamete production, transport of nutrients and waste products by archeocytes that can move freely through the mesohyl.

Cell Types in Sponges

Although many different cell types are present in sponges, only two types of organ-like structures can be defined: pinacocytes forming a pinacoderm and choanocytes forming choanocyte chambers. The other cell types are scattered through the mesohyl.

Archeocytes are the most prominent cells in the mesohyl. Besides transport through the sponge and digestion of nutrients, they have the capacity to differentiate into any other cell type. They provide a regulatory mechanism establishing and maintaining the equilibrium between different cell types. Some capacity for further development is retained by choanocytes, which can form gametes and by collencytes, which can become pinacocytes or myocytes.

The sponge skeleton is built by collencytes, spongocytes and sclerocytes. Collencytes secrete dispersed fibrillar collagen, while spongocytes build a complex supportive collagen matrix (spongin), which is the framework for the sponge. Spicula are often embedded in the collagenous matrix. The production of spicules occurs inside specialised cells, the sclerocytes, where silica or calcite is deposited in an organised way.

Finally, there are also many cell types containing small granules or vesicles. All these cells types can be grouped as granulocytes. A large number of different functions is attributed to the different granulocyte cell types. They have been), unconventional sterols , pigments or glycogen. In addition some granulocytes release components that comprise the mesohyl, like mucous or lectins (Bretting et al., 1983). Moreover, there are many more sponge-cell types (e.g. porocytes, lophocytes, myocytes, bacteriocytes, trophocytes or thesocytes). Their more specialised roles in sponge physiology will not be discussed here.

Associated Organisms

Other cell types that can be very abundant in sponges are microorganisms, such as bacteria, algae, cyanobacteria, fungi or other unicellular organisms, such as thraustochytrids Traditionally, the role of symbionts was considered to be related to their ability to recycle nutrients, or in the case of cyanobacteria and other chemoautotrophic bacteria, to supplement the diet of the sponge by fixing carbon and nitrogen, while the sponge provides its guests with a substratum for attachment and with nutrients. Another role of symbionts in sponges is the production of bioactive compounds, such as antibiotics, antifungal compounds and compounds that prevent predation or fouling. Symbionts are mainly located in the mesohyl, and especially bacteria can be numerous in some sponges, occupying up to 40% of the mesohyl volume. Lectins, which are a major constituent of the mesohyl, mediate sponge-cell attachment to the mesohyl matrix and it has been suggested that they can also play a role in the specific interactions between the sponge and its symbionts in the mesohyl.

Pseudomonas insoluta, a bacterium inhabiting the marine sponge Halichondria panicea, could only be cultured in the presence of Halichondria panicea lectin. Other lectins could not induce growth of the bacterium, while the Halichondrian lectin did not support the growth of bacteria isolated from six other marine sponges . In addition, it was found that different sponge species in the same area contain different bacterial populations However, more recently, molecular evidence suggested that sponges have a relatively uniform microbial community in the mesohyl. In addition, intracellular bacteria have been found in sponges. They are present within large vacuoles of archeocytes, which are termed bacteriocytes. However, there is still only very little information on the nature of these associations.

Reproduction

Sponges are capable of both asexual and sexual reproduction The most simple way of reproduction is fragmentation of a sponge, for example due to heavy wave action. The dispersal of such sponge fragments can lead to reattachment and establishment of new individuals. Budding is a process that is comparable with fragmentation, with the difference that budding is controlled by the sponge. Buds begin as thin filaments, which contain a few spicules in their core, at the exterior of the sponge or in the walls of oscules. These filaments then develop a distal swelling, some 5 mm in diameter. Subsequently, the buds drop off and round up. The current in the sea can transport them to a new location, where they can attach to a substratum and develop into a new functional sponge. The outside of buds is covered by exopinacocytes and numerous collagen-secreting cells. The interior of buds consists mainly of archeocytes geanulocytes and collencytes.

Some sponges form gemmules as survival structures. Gemmules are small spheres, which range in size from about 300 up to 1000 µm. They have an outer spongin coat, which generally contains spicules and an inner mass of yolk-laden cells (thesocytes). The formation of gemmules starts with the aggregation of archeocytes in the mesohyl of the sponge). Archeocytes arriving early develop into thesocytes and contain nutrients to support development into a new sponge. Archeocytes arriving later differentiate into spongocytes and form a spongin sheath on the exterior of the gemmule . Spicules can be inserted in the spongin layer in a random fashion Gemmules are located at the base of the sponge and remain attached to the substrate after the sponge has died. Fully formed gemmules are kept in a quiescent state by low temperature (3-4°C) or in the presence of the inhibitor gemmulostasin.

Gemmulostasin is produced by the parent tissue and inhibits the germination of these gemmules. However when the parent sponge disintegrates, gemmules can start to germinate. Germination starts with the outflow of the thesocytes through a narrow opening. They spread out on the gemmule coat and the substratum and attach. Within a week after germination, spicules, canals and choanocyte chambers are formed and a functional sponge is developed.

Although they are fixed to a substratum, a number of different sexual reproductive processes exist in sponges. In general, sponges are hermaphrodite, but produce oocytes and spermatocytes at different times. Spermatocytes are formed by differentiation of choanocytes, while for oocytes, both archeocytes and choanocytes have been described as stem cells. Oocytes are located in the mesohyl of 'female' sponges and need to be fertilised *in situ*. 'Smoking sponges' emit clouds of sperm from the oscules over periods up to 20 min. Spermatozoa can be taken into the 'female' sponge via the inflowing water. They are captured in the choanocyte chambers and enter the mesohyl to locate the oocytes.

Subsequently, embryogenesis is initiated and a number of cleavages takes place. The embryo is transformed into a ciliated mature larva in a few steps It is usually considered that larvae are released via the oscules before they swim a 3-48 hours in the sea. Prior to attachment the larvae enter a short creeping phase. After attachment the larvae quickly become functional young sponges.

In addition, the sexual products of some demosponges develop directly into small perfect young sponges without an intervening larval stage, which can also be released via the oscules. Fertilised oocytes can also be released, before they have developed into larvae. The time between expulsion of the eggs and development into a larva is approximately 24 hours. These larvae crawl for a period up to 20 days before they attach and differentiate into a young sponge.

Sponges as a Product

It is not exactly clear when sponges were used by humans for the first time. It goes back at least to the time of Homer, some seven hundred years before Christ. In the Iliad, he describes Hephaestus, the lame god of artists and blacksmiths, using a sponge to wash his face and body after working at the forge. In the Odyssey, he writes that when the suitors of Penelope had dined, white-armed maidens cleared the food and washed down the table with sponges. In the bible, it is described that Jesus Christ asked for some water when he suffered on the cross, but the Roman centurions gave him a sponge soaked in bile and vinegar instead. On the Greek island of Kalymnos, which has been the centre of commercial bath sponge business during the last centuries, the sponge divers used to say that Jesus Christ had cursed that sponge and from that time, sponges were sent to the deepest seas and it was ordained that men would suffer in bringing them to land. The first sponges that were obtained were also not taken from the sea floor, but they were sponges that were drifted ashore and collected by the Phoenicians. Greek divers started harvesting sponges from the sea and in the 19th and 20th century natural bathing sponge trade became big business Sponges have been used for numerous applications: cleaning, painting, filtration, or as a gas mask. Women used sponges to absorb menstrual discharge or as contraceptive. Classical bootblacks used sponges instead of a piece of cloth. Knights and soldiers used them as pad under their helmets and leg guards in order to reduce the strength of hostile pushes. The Roman emperor Caligula used sponges to sentence people to death by letting them suffocate. Burglars even tied sponges to their feet to have their steps unheard. South American and African tribes used fresh-water sponges as additive to clay for making ceramics. The sponge spicules had the function of metal wires in concrete and made ceramics less vulnerable for cracks. One sponge that does not contain spicules, Chondrosia reniformis, was eaten raw, roasted or cooked by Dalmatian fisherman Nowadays most natural sponges have been replaced by synthetic ones or other devices and natural sponges are regarded as a luxury product or even as an oddity or just for decoration.

Sponges and Biotechnology

Currently, sponges have gained renewed interest due to many secondary metabolites with potential pharmaceutical applications that have been discovered. Some of them, such as manoalide and halichondrin B were harvested in large quantities for clinical trials However, the combination of predominantly low concentrations of these molecules and the low growth rates of sponges in the sea results in a very slow production of the bioactive compounds. For *Lissodendoryx* sp., the sponge species containing the highest halichondrin B concentration (400 µg/kg), it was estimated that for the production of a medicine to treat patients with melanoma, a total of 5000 tonnes of sponge would be required. In addition, it was estimated that only approximately 300 tonnes are present in the seas The halichondrin B case is not an exceptional example and therefore, other methods to obtain large quantities of sponge metabolites have gained attention in the last decade. Researchers have explored a range of possible ways:

1. *Mariculture:* cultivation of sponges on designated areas in the sea.
2. *Ex situ culture:* cultivation of sponges under controlled conditions outside of the sea.
3. Cell and tissue culture.
4. Chemical synthesis of the metabolites or analogues.

Production of the sponge metabolites by a genetically modified host is not included in this list, as there is currently only very little information about the genes that are involved in the pathways that lead to the production of the bioactive compounds.

Index

❑❑❑